I0754780

FROM DREAMS TO DRIVE

TRUST GOD'S PLAN, EMBRACE YOUR GIFTS, AND WALK IN PURPOSE

TANESHIA YERBY
FOUNDER OF CHRISTIAN ENTREPRENEUR ORGANIZATION®

ZONDERVAN

From Dreams to Drive

Published by Zondervan, 3950 Sparks Drive SE, Suite 101, Grand Rapids, Michigan 49546, USA. by Zondervan. Zondervan is a registered trademark of The Zondervan Corporation, L.L.C., a wholly owned subsidiary of HarperCollins Christian Publishing, Inc. Requests for information should be addressed to customercare@harpercollins.com..

ISBN 9780310466789 (HC)
ISBN 9780310466802 (audiobook)
ISBN 9780310466796 (eBook)

HarperCollins Publishers, Macken House, 39/40 Mayor Street Upper, Dublin 1, D01 C9W8, Ireland (https://www.harpercollins.com)

Published in association with the literary agency of April 23rd Agency.

Art direction and cover design: Sabryna Lugge
Interior design: Emily Ghattas
Photography (back cover): Jontell Vanessa Photography

Printed in Vietnam

25 26 27 28 29 SEV 10 9 8 7 6 5 4 3 2 1

To my parents, who taught me to seek the Lord with my whole heart. You showed me what it means to walk in grace and strength, and your example continues to guide me every day. I am forever grateful for the foundation you laid.

To my three beautiful daughters, Olivia, Sydney, and Nevaeh—the best bonus daughter I ever could've asked for. You are a constant reminder of God's goodness in my life. Each of you inspires me in your own unique way, and it is a privilege beyond words to be your mother. This book is as much yours as it is mine. May you always know the depth of my love and the power of God's grace in our lives.

To my cousin Christina, you were truly one of one. A smile bright enough to light up any room, a vibrant personality that never met a stranger, and a soul that was wise beyond your years. Thank you for always seeing me—for believing in me. Cousin night will never be the same without you, but we'll do our best to hold on to the beautiful memories we shared. Steen bean, I love you and miss you dearly.

CONTENTS

PART 2: GET COMFORTABLE BEING UNCOMFORTABLE

PUSH PAST FEAR AND STEP INTO YOUR CALLING

PART 3: IDENTIFY HOMEGROWN HURDLES

MANAGE THE EMOTIONAL WEIGHT OF PURSUING YOUR PURPOSE

PART 4: FIND THE COURAGE TO MOVE FORWARD

EMBRACE THE UNKNOWN AND TRUST GOD'S PLAN

INTRODUCTION

Every woman hits a point in life when she knows God is calling her to more. Problem is, sometimes we don't quite know what that *more* is, much less how to get there.

That's the exact reason I wrote this book. I know what it's like to feel anxious about your future or frustrated when things just aren't clicking, or to lack the confidence to try something new. I've experienced it all, and I want to offer you hope that there's something beautiful waiting on the other side of your obedience.

You'll hear me say this more than once because I know it to be true: God will never give you an assignment that He doesn't intend to help you achieve. That's not just a cute quote that *sounds* good—it's God's truth.

It's easy to believe everyone else has it together or that they've never experienced struggles, but that couldn't be further from the truth. We all have our own unique experiences when it comes to discovering our purpose, and in this book, I'm sharing some of my own personal stories. I pray that they allow you to see how God's timing is perfect and how He is always aligning the pieces. Not just in my life, but in *yours* too.

You can feel scared,
but you're still called.
You can feel unqualified,
but you're still called.
You can feel unworthy,
but you're still called.

And I'll be honest: I didn't always have that perspective. I've had countless seasons when I felt like I had nothing to offer the world or that I was unqualified to pursue the tasks God had placed in front of me. Yet each time God reminded me that my feelings were not facts.

Because here's the thing:

You can feel scared, but you're still called.

You can feel unqualified, but you're still called.

You can feel unworthy, but you're still called.

How you *feel* doesn't negate the call that God has placed on your life.

And here's another thing I've learned: None of us are exempt from being put in uncomfortable situations. There will always be something that God places in front of us that forces us to level up. What good would it do for Him to allow us to stay in our comfort zone? What good would it do for Him to not push us to pursue the very thing He *created* us to do?

God doesn't promise us that the journey will be easy—just that it'll be worth it. When you step out of your comfort zone and start pursuing the call God has given you, don't be moved by the challenges that may come, because there's nothing He can't help you overcome. Some may call it crazy, but others? We call it faith.

My prayer for you is that, through this book, you'll recognize any roadblocks that are hindering your progress and you'll get comfortable being uncomfortable when taking leaps of faith. I want to show you how to manage your emotions in a way that gives you the courage to trust that God won't let you hit the ground. And when things look (and feel) like they're not working out, I want you to have faith to still move forward.

By the end of this book, you should have fully adopted the CEO mindset—where you **consider** God's Word before allowing any negative thoughts to become a breeding ground, where you **examine** and hold yourself accountable to the role you play in your own success, and where you petition God through prayer and **offer** back to Him what was already His to begin with (your future). Overall, I hope this journey helps you have a better understanding of what God is calling you to do.

Trust me when I say this: Each one of us has a unique assignment, even if we don't know what it is yet. Ten years ago I never would've guessed that my assignment would be creating and leading Christian Entrepreneur Organization (CEO)—a community for women of faith looking to fulfill their God-given purpose—but here we are. Even when I didn't know it, God was nudging me in the direction I needed to go to make it happen. So even if you don't know now what mark you're called to leave on this world, keep moving forward. You will one day.

Your **gifts** are not **random**.

Your gifts are not random.

Those ideas you just can't seem to shake aren't either.

Whatever God is calling you to pursue, He is nudging you toward it, and He has already equipped you to do it.

Cheers to you for being bold and answering the call. This is only the beginning.

With love,

TANESHIA

PART 1

FOLLOW GOD'S BLUEPRINT

THE FOUNDATION OF YOUR GIFTS

Do you ever sit back and wonder how your life is going to play out? What career you might have—or whether you will switch to a new one? What life will look like ten years from now? Whether you'll ever feel truly fulfilled? Whether those big dreams will ever become a reality? Whether you'll ever actually know your God-given purpose?

Well, I do.

Maybe you struggle with putting your plan in motion. Or maybe you're worried that you'll try something new and fail. Or perhaps you feel overwhelmed with the vision God has placed in your heart, and you're afraid you won't be able to live up to your full potential.

Yep, I've been there too.

We go through so many thoughts and emotions when it comes to planning for the future, especially when we want to live a life that's in alignment with God's plans. I'll be honest, old me used to sit and worry about the future—a lot. Now I've come to understand that each piece of the journey is important (even the not-so-good moments), and the plans we come up with for ourselves don't even come close to what God has in store for us. God's plan is the ultimate blueprint.

If you've ever done a puzzle, then you know that the typical approach to putting it together is to begin with the border and then work your way inward. As you fill in the middle pieces, the picture starts to take shape. You see that the random-looking pieces weren't so random after all but were in fact part of the bigger picture. Much like a puzzle, nothing about your life is random, including your gifts and your purpose. There is something so much bigger that God is orchestrating in your life, but sometimes you can see only a glimpse of what He's doing.

Throughout the first part of this book, I'm going to challenge you to zoom out and look at the bigger picture—whether you already know what God is calling you to do or you're still trying to figure it out. We'll cover everything from having the courage to take those big (hard) questions to God, to learning how to identify your gifts, to understanding why it's important to use your gifts to serve others, and more. Don't let one small part of your story force you into creating a false narrative about yourself or your entire future. Truth is, you have a purpose, you have gifts, and you have something that the world desperately needs. We're all rooting for you.

1

I'VE GOT QUESTIONS

I will never forget that night. It was around 3:00 a.m., and for some reason, my daughter, who was three at the time, was restless. Every twenty minutes or so, she'd peek her head in our bedroom just to say she couldn't sleep. I remember staring up at the ceiling and wondering to myself, *What's going on tonight?* And just as I finished my thought, I heard God say, *It's Me. I want to talk*.

I hopped out of bed, raced downstairs, grabbed my anointing oil, and began praying. For God's voice to be *that* clear, this had to be serious. A few moments later, that quiet voice came again: *Ask Me for what you want*.

I spent the next few minutes pretty much telling God how

angry I was that I hadn't figured out my life's purpose yet. I just couldn't understand how I could have these gifts, talents, and big dreams, yet none of them seemed to be working to bring me the success I'd hoped for.

Asking God the **right questions** is sometimes the **bridge** between where you are and where **you want to be**.

I was spending hours every day trying to prove to God, myself, and others how badly I wanted it, but it seemed like no matter what I did, I wasn't getting any results. Then it hit me: I was so blinded by chasing success with my own plans that I hadn't even considered whether I was in alignment with God's plans for me or what success looked like in His eyes.

As I was about to go on a tangent about what I felt was going wrong in my life, I stopped and asked, "What do *You* want from *me*?"

When God answered, it was simple yet powerful: *I just want your voice.* In that moment, I finally understood that asking God the right questions is sometimes the bridge between where you are and where you want to be.

God isn't being secretive about what He desires from you, nor is He hiding from you. Sometimes there is just a lack of communication on your part.

Matthew 7:7–8 says that if you *seek*, you will *find*, and if you knock, the door will be opened. So whatever it is you need, you can be assured that when you bring it to God, it'll be revealed to you. Whether it's finding out what your gifts are, praying for a creative breakthrough in your ideas, or even knowing what steps to take to see progress on your journey, who better to ask these questions than the One who created you?

Open your mouth, ask the hard (but necessary) questions, and **trust** that everything else will fall into place—**because it will**.

Your dreams and your destiny are not a DIY project—you do not have to "do it yourself." Yes, you will be the one taking action, but you don't have to be the one who creates the entire plan from scratch—God already did that *when He created you*. Open your mouth, ask the hard (but necessary) questions, and trust that everything else will fall into place—because it will.

CONSIDER

"Don't bargain with God. Be direct. Ask for what you need. This isn't a cat-and-mouse, hide-and-seek game we're in. If your child asks for bread, do you trick him with sawdust? If he asks for fish, do you scare him with a live snake on his plate? As bad as you are, you wouldn't think of such a thing. You're at least decent to your own children. So don't you think the God who conceived you in love will be even better?"

Matthew 7:7–11 MSG

EXAMINE

Have you been honest with God about what you're struggling with in this season? Have you been still enough to hear His voice?

....

....

....

OFFER

God, I know that You created me with a purpose in mind, and I pray that I never lose sight of that. I ask that You continue to guide my steps and give me the wisdom to handle all that You've called me to pursue. In Jesus' name, amen.

2

COINCIDENCE OR CALLING?

It was my college orientation, and as I sat in the auditorium with hundreds of other students, a faculty member asked each of us to raise our hand when we heard our major being called out. At that time I was still unsure what I wanted to pursue, so I quietly looked around the room at my peers, watching and waiting to see what they'd choose. When they announced the mass communications program, I could instantly feel the excitement—and that was all it took for me to choose that major.

Silly, I know. Sharing this story fifteen years ago came with a lot of embarrassment, but as I've grown I've come to realize that what I thought was a random, impulsive decision was me hearing God's voice and acting on it—without hesitation.

I'd always had dreams of being on stage one day, yet I was extremely shy. Unless you were a close family member or friend, I didn't have much to say. Being in that communications program forced me to speak up—literally. I had to learn the art of storytelling, how to capture an audience's attention, and how to write and produce my own news segments. I didn't realize it in the moment, but the work I was doing was slowly building my confidence for what I do today.

God knows where to place each of us in every season of our lives. The things we experience that we may consider coincidences are likely God orchestrating the pieces so we can walk in our true purpose. We are so busy looking for a big reveal that we don't even recognize that God is showing us in real time the path He wants us to take. Sometimes He'll give you gentle nudges long before He shows you *big* signs.

We are so busy looking for a **big reveal** that we don't even recognize that **God is showing us** in real time the **path** He wants us to take.

Like sending people your way who need help or advice with a specific problem.

Or dropping an idea in your mind, year after year after year.

Or putting you in an auditorium full of wild college students to help inspire your major.

The nudges are always there, both big and small. It's up to you to slow down and become present to see how God is lighting your path and directing you in the way you should go.

The nudges are always there, both big and small. It's up to you to **slow down** and become present to see how God is **lighting your path** and directing you in the way you should go.

If you're feeling like you can't quite put your finger on the thing God is calling you to do, take a step back and identify common themes:

- Something I love doing is . . .
- Something that shows up in my life over and over again is . . .
- Something others think I'm good at is . . .

God put those things there for a reason. Your purpose and gifts are already within you. They're just waiting to be discovered.

CONSIDER

"Before I formed you in the womb I knew you, before you were born I set you apart; I appointed you as a prophet to the nations."

Jeremiah 1:5 NIV

EXAMINE

When was the last time you slowed down to take inventory of your gifts? Do you ever mistake God's gentle nudges for mere coincidence?

....

....

....

....

OFFER

God, I pray that You open my eyes so I can see my future and my purpose the way You see it. I pray that You open my heart to be obedient to Your gentle nudges, and that You would help me move in the direction You are calling me to go. I thank You for going before me and lighting up my path every step of the way. In Jesus' name, amen.

3

IT'S ALL IN THE DETAILS

As a child, I spent a lot of time reading and writing. I still rode bikes and played with toys, but getting lost in a book? That was my thing. I had a small flashlight I'd hide in my nightstand so I could read books after bedtime. The light must've shone through the space between the floor and the bottom of my door because my mom would always catch me red-handed.

I'd spend my weekends "self-publishing" my own books. My mom and I would bind them together with cardboard, a tiny glue gun, and fancy wrapping paper to finish them off. I was so proud of those self-published books that I

How often do you **overlook** the things **you do with ease**?

wrote them for family and friends and passed them out as gifts. Talk about confidence!

Think about your own story for a moment. How often do you overlook the things you do with ease? For whatever reason, we sometimes associate *ease* with having little value. Consider our breathing, walking, and talking. Because most of us do these things with such ease and so often, over time we lose sight of the fact that each one is a true blessing from God. And if any of these things were ever taken away, we would immediately notice their significance.

What if we looked at our gifts and talents this way? What if we stopped brushing them off as mere coincidence or hobbies and treated them as something God intentionally gave us? Maybe you're like I was back then, and you don't know much about gifts or purpose or how to identify them. Maybe you're expecting purpose to be something difficult, or maybe you're thrown off by the fact that things just flow with ease.

Now is a good time to revisit your list from the last section—the tasks you love to do, the moments that appear over and over, the times when others seek you out for a specific task. Are any of these particularly easy for you? Can you see God's intentionality in these gifts?

Little Taneshia was already an author in her head long before she knew anything about purpose or becoming a published author. During my childhood, reading and writing just seemed like fun hobbies. Yet the reason this came with ease is because it was a God-given gift and it's what I was created to do.

There are no coincidences when it comes to God and His plan for you. Everything He does is intentional.

There are **no coincidences** when it comes to God and **His plan** for you.

Everything.

From how He created heaven and earth to how He created you with a specific purpose in mind before placing you in your mother's womb. Since the beginning of time God has paid attention to even the *smallest* of details—including the gifts and ideas that He placed inside you. Even the thing that seems small or too easy has a purpose. Don't overlook it.

CONSIDER

The LORD directs the steps of the godly. He delights in every detail of their lives.

Psalm 37:23 NLT

EXAMINE

What gifts might you have overlooked now or in your past? How can you take action and use them wisely?

....

....

....

....

....

OFFER

God, help me not to overlook the gifts You have deposited within me. I know that You are intentional with all things, including me. I pray for wisdom, confidence, and clarity as I show up and pursue what You've created me to do. I thank You in advance for guiding my steps. In Jesus' name, amen.

4

YOUR GIFTS AREN'T JUST FOR YOU

Every year on Christmas Eve my family hosts a big dinner. We play games, laugh, eat way too much food, and enjoy each other's company. This has been a family tradition since I was a child, and it's wild to think that we've been able to keep it up for nearly forty years.

Like most Christmas parties, we do an annual gift exchange. It started out as a simple name draw exchange, but more recently has shifted to a white elephant exchange. Essentially, everyone brings a wrapped gift, all participants draw a number, everyone forms a circle around the pile of gifts, and we begin the gift draw from the smallest number to the largest. The thing that catches most first-time participants off guard is that the gift you select can be taken from you. It gets pretty rowdy (in a fun way), and in the end, no one should end up with the gift they brought—that would defeat the purpose of the game. You buy it to *give* it, not *keep* it.

Pursuing your purpose is obviously a lot different from participating in a white elephant gift exchange, but would you believe me if I told you that the same rules apply in life? Your gifts aren't for you to keep; they're for the people connected to you. It's not that you won't benefit from your gifts or even find enjoyment in using them (because you will), but the truth of the matter is that God gives us gifts so we can leave a positive impact on the world.

Your **gifts** aren't for you to keep; they're **for the people** connected to you.

When we hold on to our gifts, we're not using them to their full potential and reaching the people that God has called us to serve. Not only does that go against the very thing God has instructed us to do, but there's a lot more at stake than meets the eye.

Here's what you may not have considered:

> There's somebody out there waiting to hear your story.

There's somebody out there waiting for you to
minister to them.
There's somebody out there waiting to read
your book.
There's somebody out there waiting to ignite *their*
fire with a spark from *your* flame.

Before you ask yourself, *Why me?* remember that everyone has their own unique gifts. Even if you were to take multiple people with similar gifts, the reality is no one can do what you do in the way you do it.

The way you talk.

The way you write.

The way you sing.

The way you minister.

Your unique abilities cannot be duplicated. Someone can come close, but they'll never be an exact replica. And if you ever find yourself saying that you're not qualified, remember that God does not call the qualified; He qualifies those He calls—and that includes *you*.

Remember that God does not call the qualified; He qualifies those He calls—and **that includes you**.

CONSIDER

Each of you should use whatever gift you have received to serve others, as faithful stewards of God's grace in its various forms.

1 Peter 4:10 NIV

EXAMINE

Do you truly believe that others can benefit from you using your gifts? Explain your answer.

....

....

....

OFFER

God, You have entrusted me with these gifts to leave a positive impact on the world. I pray that You will help me use them in a way that is pleasing to You. I know that my obedience is tied to someone else's breakthrough, so I ask that You give me the courage and motivation to keep showing up. Even when I don't feel qualified, I pray that You will remind me that I am still called and equipped. In Jesus' name, amen.

5

BE PATIENT

My grandmother had a small garden when I was growing up. I was fascinated by the idea of being self-sufficient and able to live off your own land. During a slower season in my adult life, I figured it was as good a time as any to get into gardening. I mean, how hard could it be?

It didn't take my husband, Tre, long to get everything ready. Within a week, we started planting seeds and patiently waited to see the progress. Every day for weeks, my daughters and I would look through the back window to see if anything was sprouting. But there was nothing—not a single sprout. We fussed over the garden, trying to figure out where we'd gone wrong. Perhaps we'd gotten the wrong fertilizer? Maybe bugs were eating the new sprouts? Maybe our plants weren't getting enough sunlight?

While we waited for our garden to grow, our lives got busy again. We started spending less time at home, tending to our garden less and less. We stopped watering, fighting the insects, and checking on its progress altogether. Eventually we tore the garden down.

Sometimes you need to **take your focus off waiting** for the fruit and just **focus on the gardening**.

To our surprise, several weeks later we had lettuce sprouting up all over our forgotten garden. I guess we had done something right after all.

How often do we do this with our dreams and goals? We plant the seeds, water them, and tend them until we get too tired to keep up, and then we let them go. And the crazy thing is, sometimes we let go right before a big breakthrough.

Sometimes you need to take your focus off waiting for the fruit and just focus on the gardening.

- Start using your gifts even when you have a small audience.
- Start sharing your story even when you're not sure if it'll resonate with anyone.
- Start pursuing those ideas even if they seem too far out of your reach.

God can do a whole lot with effort and obedience.

What we often overlook is that while we are the ones planting the seeds, it's God work behind the scenes that makes them grow. Although we may not be able to see immediate growth, the seeds that we are planting are taking root to grow into something bigger than we can imagine. Whatever that is won't produce fruit too soon, and it won't produce it too late. It'll grow right on time, exactly when it's supposed to.

Fun fact: It takes nearly twenty to fifty years for an oak tree to reach maturity. How crazy is that? That means it takes decades of watering before an acorn finally becomes what it's supposed to be. The seeds that you plant and water today could very well be the beginning of something big in the future.

The **seeds that you plant and water** today could very well be the beginning of **something big in the future**.

As challenging as it might be, don't ever stop watering your seeds and tending to your garden. Those gifts and ideas that God has placed in your heart are there for a reason. Something might be growing in the spiritual realm long before it produces tangible fruit that you can see, but hang tight—it's coming.

CONSIDER

So neither the one who plants nor the one who waters is anything, but only God, who makes things grow. The one who plants and the one who waters have one purpose, and they will each be rewarded according to their own labor. For we are co-workers in God's service; you are God's field, God's building.

1 Corinthians 3:7–9 NIV

EXAMINE

What seeds have you left unattended? How can you be a good steward of the gifts that God has entrusted to you?

....

....

....

OFFER

Lord, I pray that You give me patience while I'm in a season of planting seeds. No matter how long it takes, help me to be a good steward of the gifts and ideas You have called me to pursue. I know that when the time is right, You will make sure that all Your promises are fulfilled. In Jesus' name, amen.

PART 1 WRAP-UP

ACTION PLAN TO FOLLOW GOD'S BLUEPRINT

Sis, we've just started this journey to uncover the foundation of your gifts and follow God's blueprint, but we're going to pause here to make sure things are really setting in. So far we've learned the importance of asking God hard questions, paying attention to the details, and using our gifts to serve others. Now it's time to put what you've learned into action. On the next pages are three action steps to help you identify areas that may be affecting the way you show up. Don't feel rushed to answer everything right away. The goal is to spend time on each step and get to the root of any issues.

STEP #1: WHAT QUESTIONS HAVE YOU BEEN AVOIDING ASKING GOD?

Are you avoiding these questions because you don't think He'll answer? Or because you feel guilty for not already knowing the answer? Is it because you don't know how (or what) to ask? Is it because you don't have a personal relationship with Him? Once you can identify the questions you've been avoiding and the reasoning behind it, you can move forward toward getting the clarity you need to pursue your life's purpose.

STEP #2: IDENTIFY THE WAYS THAT YOU CAN USE YOUR GIFTS TO SERVE OTHERS. ARE YOU ALREADY DOING THIS? IF NOT, EXPLAIN.

Sometimes we lose sight of how impactful our gifts can be to those we are called to serve. We do ourselves and our communities a disservice when we hoard or hide the thing that God has called us to share abundantly with others. Even if you don't know how everything will play out in the end, use your gifts and allow God to handle the rest. Are you already doing this? If not, explain why.

STEP #3: ARE YOU EVER HESITANT TO KEEP WATERING YOUR SEEDS WHEN YOU DON'T SEE IMMEDIATE GROWTH? WHY?

Take inventory of how much time passes before you become frustrated and give up. Sometimes we put so much unnecessary pressure on ourselves when our goal should be simply to plant the seeds and allow God to make them grow.

PART 2

GET COMFORTABLE BEING UNCOMFORTABLE

PUSH PAST FEAR AND STEP INTO YOUR CALLING

Before we jump into identifying your true purpose, I want you to consider this: God allows us to have different experiences in life that may not always *feel* good in the moment, but these things are necessary for our growth. Think of it as His way of preparing us.

What if all your challenging moments in life are part of a bigger picture? What if their sole purpose is to move you closer to the thing that God is calling you to do? Even when the opportunities aren't showing up like you expected or the ideas aren't sticking or you're not getting the support you thought you'd have, you can find hope in knowing that God's promises will still be fulfilled in your life.

That doesn't mean the journey will be easy, and it's most certainly not an invitation to quit at the first sign of a challenge. In fact, you should probably anticipate a few bumps along the way. Not every challenge is a sign that you're doing something wrong; sometimes difficulties are proof that you're trying and, through the process of elimination, discovering what works and what doesn't.

We have two choices in life: Number one is to remember

that we are capable of doing whatever God calls us to do (and then actually *do it*). Number two is to throw in the towel and bow out gracefully. My job is to make sure you have the tools you need to keep moving forward.

In this next section, we're going to talk about what it looks like to step out in faith, shift your mindset toward challenges, and trust that if God calls you, He'll equip you.

You may not currently see how everything will unfold, but that doesn't mean pieces aren't falling into place. Your job is to keep showing up and allow your life experiences to help you put the pieces together. Remember, life and purpose are like a puzzle, and what you're working on is a masterpiece. Just wait and see.

6

CHAPTERS OF LIFE

When I was younger I loved reading. But as I grew older and took on more responsibilities, it became harder to find free time to read. A few years ago a family member gifted me a novel to help reignite my love for reading. One book led to another, and before I knew it, I was a self-proclaimed bookworm again.

Everything usually **comes together** in the end.

As I have reengaged with reading, something has stood out to me with every story: No matter how riveting the overall plot of a book may be, there are often a few chapters that aren't exciting. It's not that they're boring or even unnecessary; they just don't have the same thrill as the others. And here's what else I realized: Everything usually comes together in the end.

The same can be said about the story of our lives. Some chapters are full of excitement, and we're so clear about the direction we're heading, while other chapters are full of ebbs and flows, and we can barely understand what's happening.

Maybe it's taking forever to develop that business idea.

Or we're being overlooked and feeling left out.

It could be that we're doing the work but not making the progress that we expected.

And if we're not careful, before long, we start treating a challenging season as if it's the be-all and end-all. We start losing hope for the things that we were praying for, we become more and more disappointed, and we lose hope that better days are ahead.

But what if we treated those less exciting chapters of life like we do a good novel? When we know the ending of the story will be good, so not only do we keep reading, but we *expect* that it's all going to work out in the end. What if we didn't put too much emphasis on the disappointment that one chapter might bring because we know that the *overall story* that God has planned for our lives is good?

The Bible tells us that God sees all and knows all because He orchestrated it from the very beginning. Isaiah 46:10 (NLT) says, "Only I can tell you the future before it even happens. Everything I plan will come to pass." He is in control of every chapter of life that we go through. He's just as present in the hills as He is in the valleys.

So what does that mean for you and me? It means that no matter where we are in life, we are to trust that our best days are ahead of us.

No matter where we are in life, we are to **trust** that **our best days are ahead** of us.

I know that's easier said than done. Yes, you may hit a few plot twists along the way, but that's to be expected. This is your life story, and it's still unfolding. You may not see the light at the end of the tunnel right now, but trust me, it's there. You just have to keep moving forward. What God has in store for you will more than exceed your expectations.

CONSIDER

Count it all joy, my brothers, when you meet trials of various kinds, for you know that the testing of your faith produces steadfastness. And let steadfastness have its full effect, that you may be perfect and complete, lacking in nothing.

James 1:2–4 ESV

EXAMINE

How would you describe this current season of your life? What is one thing you are expecting God to do?

....

....

....

OFFER

God, I thank You for all the chapters of my life—the good ones, the not-so-good ones, and even the unexpected twists and turns. I know that You make no mistakes, so I trust that everything I'm experiencing will turn out for my good. I pray that You help me to remain hopeful during the wait, because I know that better days are just around the corner. In Jesus' name, amen.

7

REACH BEYOND YOUR COMFORT ZONE

For my twenty-first birthday, my best friend thought it would be a good idea to surprise me with a trip to Miami. Initially I was excited, but then I realized I'd have to fly alone for the first time—including a connecting flight in Atlanta, the busiest airport in the US! How on earth was I going to get through that airport alone?

Everything went smoothly during my first flight, but as the pilot came over the intercom in preparation for landing, my nerves started getting the best of me. I contemplated staying put instead of catching my connecting flight.

Then it hit me: Even if *I* didn't make my transfer to Miami, my checked bags *would*. My best friend and all the birthday celebrations would still be in Miami, whether *I* made it there or not.

This is exactly how it is in life sometimes. God gives us instructions to do something, whether it's using our gifts, relocating to a new city, or even applying for a new job, and once we take the initial leap, we get comfortable and don't anticipate any change *beyond* that. The moment that God says, "It's time for your next move," we allow fear to overcome our thoughts.

Get **comfortable** with being uncomfortable.

But what if everything God promised you is waiting at your next stop? What if the only way to get there is to be obedient and take the next leap of faith?

It's an honest human reaction to want to stick with what's familiar, because fear of the unknown often seems like too big of a giant to defeat—especially since we don't know what's waiting on the other side. But even though *we* may not know, we must remember that God does. He sees all and knows all, and He will never lead us to a place we'll have to navigate on our own.

So get comfortable with being uncomfortable. There will always be something that God asks of you that doesn't necessarily make sense at first, but that initial step between comfort and obedience is where He does His best work.

Here's my advice: Don't wait until your back is against the wall and you're forced to take a leap of faith. Take the next step the moment God tells you to move. Don't give the Enemy the satisfaction of seeing you hesitate because this next level that God is calling you to is going to require your full yes.

What if **everything God promised you** is waiting for you at your next stop?

I know it would be much easier to stick to what you know, but you'll miss out on so much more if you don't take that leap. And you don't have to be fearless to take that next step. You just need to trust God and take one step at a time. Not only will He get you to the place you're supposed to be, but He'll make sure everything that He has in store for you is ready and waiting with your name on it.

CONSIDER

Faith is what makes real the things we hope for. It is proof of what we cannot see.

Hebrews 11:1 ERV

EXAMINE

Have you taken any recent leaps of faith? What is your initial reaction when you think about having to move beyond your comfort zone?

....

....

....

....

....

OFFER

God, I thank You for giving me the courage to move when You say move. Thank You for not allowing fear to get in the way of the bold moves that You're calling me to make. I know the journey might not be easy, but I trust that it will be worth it. In Jesus' name, amen.

8

SHOW UP

Back in high school, I was involved in more sports and extracurricular activities than I can count. Sometimes they were things I was genuinely interested in. Other times I pursued something because I wanted to challenge myself to learn something new. And then there were times when I just wanted an excuse to stay after school and make new friends. In any case, if there was a sign-up sheet, my name was on it. I remember signing up for my first season of track and field with the expectation that it would be like an after-school gym class. What I didn't know was that my track coach, Coach Jones, meant business. I wouldn't say it was all work and no play, but it was definitely a lot more work than I had anticipated.

After a few practices, I remember telling my dad I was

done. The rigorous training sessions were becoming too much to handle. What my dad said in that moment has stuck with me for nearly twenty years: "No. You signed up for it, and you're going to finish what you started. You have to at least see it through to the end." As angry as his response made me feel, I knew he was right. I had made a commitment to do something, and this was my first valuable lesson in sticking to the plan, *no matter what*.

Wanting confirmation that **you are in alignment** and pursuing things from God rather than self makes sense.

There will be times when God puts an idea in your heart and you'll get so into the weeds of pursuing it that you'll realize it's much more challenging than you had planned. For a lot of people, that becomes a major turning point in their journey.

You might be asking yourself, *If I'm experiencing so many challenges, how do I know if what I'm pursuing is from God?* And that's a valid question. Wanting confirmation that you are in alignment and pursuing things from God rather than self makes sense.

Here are a few things to consider when trying to confirm that you're on the right track with an idea you're chasing:

Is it aligned with your gifts?
Is it supported by Scripture?
Will it uplift and have a positive impact on others?
Has it been confirmed through prayer?

Keep in mind that God is not the author of confusion (1 Corinthians 14:33). So if the idea invites chaos and is reckless or harmful to yourself or others, it's not from God.

On the flip side, *hard* does not mean *impossible.*

So if God gives you an idea that seems impossible to achieve, trust Him and pursue it anyway.

If He gives you an idea that you don't feel qualified for, pursue it anyway.

If He gives you an idea that requires resources you don't have, trust that He will provide, and pursue it anyway.

Big ideas require big faith, and whatever God calls you to pursue, He will equip you for and give you whatever tools and resources you need to get it done.

Big ideas require **big faith**.

Don't forget that *your* obedience is tied to someone else's breakthrough.

CONSIDER

Commit to the LORD whatever you do, and he will establish your plans.

Proverbs 16:3 NIV

EXAMINE

What ideas keep popping up in your mind and heart? Do they align with God's Word, and could they have a positive impact on those you feel called to serve?

....

....

....

....

....

OFFER

God, I thank You for every idea that You have put in my heart. I ask that You make it distinctly clear which ideas are from You and which ones are my own. Help me to be obedient and stay in alignment with Your call for my life. In Jesus' name, amen.

9

UNDERSTAND GOD'S PROMISE

For years, I drove by small resale shops and thrift stores on my commute to work, but I never considered going inside any of them. As far as I remembered from my childhood, there wasn't much inside other than a few antiques, a scratch-and-dent section for well-used furniture, and clothes that probably should've been recycled or tossed rather than donated. It wasn't until I had a work trip that required me to be in full business suits for five days that I even considered stopping in, but I needed to make my money stretch.

Based on the outward appearance of the building and my preconceived notions, I wasn't expecting to find much. To my surprise, this thrift store was *a lot* different than I remembered. Full racks of clothing organized by size, shelves

How often do we **prejudge** certain assignments from God based on their **outward appearance or on a preconceived notion**?

full of housewares, lots of nice furniture—this place had it all. Not only did I find the five suits I needed, but I also found so much more.

How often do we prejudge certain assignments from God based on their outward appearance or on a preconceived notion? We don't even give ourselves the opportunity to be optimistic about what *could* be because we can't see past the surface of what's directly in front of us. And in turn, that dictates how much effort (if any) we put into pursuing the thing that God has tasked us with.

We start saying things like:

> "God, I don't know why You would give me this idea when I don't even have the resources."
>
> "God, why would You choose me to launch this ministry when others are more qualified?"
>
> "God, I have so many other responsibilities. How am I supposed to find time to get this done?"

Before we know it, we've formed a negative opinion about the very thing that God has called us to pursue without giving it a real chance to take shape.

But what would happen if you refused to prejudge the outcome based on what you can see and instead trusted God through the process? What would happen if you decided that, instead of putting your focus on what you *don't* have, you trusted that God will equip you with more than enough?

What would happen if you refused to prejudge the outcome based on what you can see and instead **trusted God** through the process?

More often than not, the assignment that God gives you won't be an easy one. Much like that thrift store, the outset of your journey may not look pretty and polished when you first find it. But as you move forward and allow God to guide your steps, you'll find hidden gems along the way.

The goal is to keep an open mind and an open heart, and to make the conscious decision to hold tight to God's promises—no matter what the present looks like. Your circumstances can go from test to testimony, just like that.

It's up to you to make a conscious decision to take God at His word and remain optimistic about what He is calling you to do. Circumstances will change, but His call on your life remains the same.

CONSIDER

Jesus replied, "You do not realize now what I am doing, but later you will understand."

John 13:7 NIV

EXAMINE

What is a task God has assigned to you that looks much different than you expected? How can you release some of those negative preconceptions that you've been storing in your heart and move forward?

....

....

....

....

....

OFFER

God, help me to keep an open mind to the things that You've called me to pursue. I know the journey may not always be easy, but I trust that the outcome will always be in my favor. In Jesus' name, amen.

10

PAVE THE WAY

When I first joined the online space, I had no clue what I was supposed to be doing. The only thing I knew was that I felt unfulfilled in life, and that God was calling me to more. At times, it felt like He was chasing me down through sleepless nights, where the only remedy was prayer, visions that reminded me of how much passion I used to have, and even God-appointed conversations that showed me I needed to rekindle the fire I once had.

Even after experiencing all those gentle nudges, I still struggled with knowing where to start. I began searching in other places for confirmation instead of letting God's instructions be enough. I was constantly looking for someone to show me the way and getting nowhere.

I reached a point where I had to trust that God would

guide my steps and give me the insight, strategies, and whatever else I needed to make it happen. After all, it was His plan, not mine. And He came through, just like He said He would.

Why am I sharing this? Because sometimes the blueprint you're looking for in others is something that God is using *you* to create. Sure, there may be others in your same industry, sharing a similar message, speaking to a similar audience, but what God has tasked you with is specific to *you*.

> Sometimes the **blueprint** you're looking for in others is something that God is using **you** to **create**.

You might find it hard to believe that God is calling you to be a pioneer. Being chosen to explore a new territory without a road map isn't for the weak. Because how on earth could you be tasked with being a pioneer in something you're not even an expert in?

But when you partner with God and allow Him to remain at the center of everything you do, you're not just operating in your own power; you're tapping into *His*. And mark my words: The strategies, creativity, resources, and relationships that start to flow to you will be more than you ever could've planned for.

When God tasks you with an assignment, let His guidance be enough. Don't waste time measuring your call against someone else's. You're not meant to do what everyone else is doing. They may be going to the left, and God is trying to send you to the right. You have a different assignment and a different group of people to impact.

Don't waste time measuring your call against someone else's.

Be okay with leading the way from where you are. Be okay with not following the crowd just for the sake of doing what already works for someone else. There is something special that God is calling you to do, and whether it's been done before is not an indication of whether it'll work for you. For all you know, God has assigned you to shift an entire industry.

Suit up for the challenge, friend. It's time to pave the way for something new.

CONSIDER

The heart of man plans his way, but the LORD establishes his steps.

Proverbs 16:9 ESV

EXAMINE

Do you feel like God is calling you to be a pioneer of something new? If so, what steps can you take to ensure that you stay focused on your assignment?

....

....

....

....

....

OFFER

God, thank You for allowing me to use my gifts to serve those connected to me. I trust that You will give me the tools and resources that I need to bring this vision to life. I pray that even when things get tough, Your voice remains the loudest in my head and in my heart. In Jesus' name, amen.

PART 2 WRAP-UP

ACTION PLAN TO GET COMFORTABLE BEING UNCOMFORTABLE

Before we move on, let's pause and do a quick recap. We've talked about the similarities between life and books, how to pave the way for something new, showing up (even when you feel defeated), and more. I hope the personal stories I've shared have made it clear that there is so much more waiting for you on the other side of your comfort zone. Being uncomfortable is a necessary part of the process. It all boils down to allowing God to lead the way and trusting that each new chapter will be better than your last.

On the following pages are three action steps that you can take to move forward with what God is calling you to do.

ACTION STEP #1: TAKE SOME TIME TO THINK ABOUT WHAT MINDSET ROADBLOCK YOU STRUGGLE WITH THE MOST.

The majority of the mindset roadblocks that we experience are a direct reflection of our past experiences. Be honest with your answer and remember: There's nothing that you can say that'll catch God by surprise.

ACTION STEP #2: WHAT IMMEDIATE CHANGES CAN YOU MAKE TO REDUCE SOME OF THOSE ROADBLOCKS?

Sometimes we experience the same mental roadblocks over and over simply because we haven't sat still long enough to get to the root of the problem in order to map out a plan to get past it.

ACTION STEP #3: DO YOU TRUST THAT YOU ARE CAPABLE OF DOING WHATEVER GOD CALLS YOU TO DO?

If yes, create a list and use it as a reminder for those days when your faith may waver. If not, why?

PART 3

IDENTIFY HOMEGROWN HURDLES

MANAGE THE EMOTIONAL WEIGHT OF PURSUING YOUR PURPOSE

Let's face it: Pursuing something outside your comfort zone can quickly begin to feel like a roller coaster. One day you're up, the next you're down, yet somehow you still find yourself with a deep desire to move forward, even through the never-ending ebbs and flows.

I'm not one of those people who will try to tell you that your emotions aren't reality or that you don't have enough faith because you experience a full range of them. I don't believe that to be true. We're human. We will naturally experience different feelings, especially when we're in unfamiliar territory—it's just part of our design. The problem isn't that we experience emotions, but rather how we *respond* to them.

> The problem isn't that we experience **emotions**, but rather how we **respond** to them.

In this next section, we'll talk about some of the emotions that come with pursuing our calling. And here's why: Something special happens when we're honest with God and call out exactly what we're feeling. He's not surprised by our emotions, and

He can not only change our situation—He can help us shift our perspective.

Speaking from experience, I've come to realize that when we're too caught up in our emotions, it's easy to miss what God is doing in our lives. We find ourselves down and out over minor setbacks, when really, it's just God repositioning us for bigger and better things. We find ourselves comparing our work to our peers', when God has called us to take up space in a completely different area. We find ourselves losing hope, not knowing that we're on the brink of our big break. This alone is enough reason to stay tapped in with God while we're on this journey.

God has designed you with a purpose that is unique to you, which means you are the *only* one who can fulfill it. There may be thousands of people out there with a similar call, but they are not *you*. And that's not said to boost your ego; it's to remind you how truly unique you are.

Don't allow your **emotions** to override your **obedience**.

So, the next time you find yourself feeling overwhelmed, I want you to remember this: Don't allow your emotions to override your obedience. Feel them, but don't sit in them.

11

AM I A FRAUD?

It had been years since I'd had a consistent workout routine. Between being busy with work, kids, and keeping my home afloat, taking care of my body was the last thing on my to-do list. It wasn't until my lack of exercise started to affect me both physically and mentally that I began to take intentional movement more seriously. If I couldn't *find* the time, I was going to have to *make* it. And that's exactly what I did.

> I was **exactly** where I was supposed to **be**.

I started walking the long parkway outside my neighborhood—two miles, every single day. I won't lie; it was brutal at first. My shins burned, the soles of my feet ached, and my breathing was labored. I was out of shape. But with every step I took, I reminded myself that it wouldn't always be this hard. Each day would get easier. I was on it with the positive affirmations.

For the first few weeks, this positive mindset worked. Then as the weather got nicer, more and more people started to use the parkway for their exercise routines. I remember watching the seasoned runners blow past me. Filled with self-doubt, I felt like an imposter trying to keep up with them. My positive thoughts instantly turned into *You don't belong out here with them* and *How did you let yourself get this out of shape?* But God quickly reminded me that I was exactly where I was supposed to be and that I wasn't giving myself enough credit for how far I had come.

If you've ever dealt with imposter syndrome, you know just how crippling it can feel. No matter how much work you've put in or how many times God has confirmed that you're walking the right path, you still feel incapable of doing some of the tasks placed in front of you.

Self-doubt sneaks up on you when you least expect it. You can be full of excitement one moment and second-guessing yourself the next. You may become overly critical or find reasons to talk yourself out of showing up. But can I tell you something? You are more capable than you give yourself credit for. God has put way too much potential inside you to let imposter syndrome be the thing that takes you out.

One of the best ways to overcome imposter syndrome is to feed yourself with God's truth. Counter every negative thought that pops up with a positive one. When I was starting my fitness journey, I would often remind myself, "I can do all things through Christ who strengthens me" (Philippians 4:13 NKJV). Find a verse that speaks to you, and memorize it. After a while, you'll start to live it. Eventually those moments of self-doubt will transform into confidence.

Oftentimes imposter syndrome is simply the result of holding ourselves to an unrealistic standard of perfection. But friend, God is not looking for perfection; He's looking for obedience.

Did you do your best? Did you put in 100 percent effort? That's enough. The people you are called to serve are not looking for perfection; they're looking for breakthrough. They won't be nearly as critical of you as you are of yourself. Can you help them overcome their struggles? Do you have personal experience in the area you're pursuing? Do you have pure intentions? Yes? That's enough.

> **Imposter syndrome** has one job: to **stop you in your tracks**.

Imposter syndrome has one job: to stop you in your tracks. If you let it win, you may never see what's on the other side of your obedience. You may

Ignore the self-doubt and **keep moving forward**.

never see all the lives that could be impacted by your gifts and ideas. You may never operate at your full capacity. It's easy to be critical of yourself, even when you're actually showing up. If you weren't doing the work, there would be nothing to discuss. There is so much to be gained when you show up in all that God has created you to be. Ignore the self-doubt and keep moving forward.

CONSIDER

For we are His workmanship, created in Christ Jesus for good works, which God prepared beforehand that we should walk in them.

Ephesians 2:10 NKJV

EXAMINE

What is one thing that you feel unqualified to do—and why? How can you overcome your self-doubt? (Perhaps take a class to sharpen your skills? Find a mentor? Spend more time perfecting your craft?)

....

....

....

....

OFFER

God, I pray that You will give me peace of mind when it comes to doing the things You've called me to do. I ask that You remove any form of imposter syndrome that is trying to distract me from being obedient. I pray that You help me be intentional with my thoughts so I can carry out my assignment. In Jesus' name, amen.

12

IS THERE TOO MUCH ON MY PLATE?

Before I started my journey to create a community for women of faith, I already had a full plate—wife, mother, and a full-time job. Adding an additional workload was a lot more than I had bargained for. It wasn't long before I started questioning if it was worth it. *Was it worth it to work myself to the bone just to pursue a dream that only God and I could see? Was it worth filling every ounce of my free time with additional tasks from my to-do list? Was it worth showing up even though it could be months, or even years, before my hard work would pay off?* Honestly, most days it felt like it wasn't. Nevertheless, I knew that if I wanted to stay in the race and do what God was calling me to do, I had to create a better work-life balance, because burnout was calling my name.

I had made the mistake of thinking that God had tasked me with stewarding only my *gifts* well, when in reality we are called to steward *everything* well—our families, our careers, and our overall health and wellness. He cares about it all. You can't neglect the other things that you have been entrusted with and still expect to find success with just the one. And as challenging as it may be to steward multiple things well, it's possible, and it's *necessary.*

Your dreams will only go so far if your personal life is falling apart.

Your dreams will only go so far if you fail to invest in your health.

Your dreams will only go so far if you neglect everything else around you.

Coming to this realization helped me create intentional balance and give my best to *all* areas of my life.

Some seasons are flat-out hard and more demanding than others, but it's important to remember that just because God gives you an idea or an assignment to pursue, that doesn't mean He's expecting you to do everything at once. More often than not, we are the ones who place these imaginary timelines on ourselves, and nine times out of ten, that plays a major part in feeling overwhelmed.

When it comes to pursuing those things that God has placed in your heart, please understand that He will never give you a task that you can't handle. Wherever He places you, He provides you the grace to handle it. And even when challenges arise and you become overwhelmed with all that's required of you, you can remember that God knows what He's doing and where He's leading you in all seasons, even the busy ones.

Just because God gives you **an idea or an assignment** to pursue, that doesn't mean He's expecting you to **do everything at once**.

Instead of ignoring what you've been called to do, pray for clarity and wisdom to make wise decisions and for the capacity to handle all that He has tasked you with in this season. It doesn't mean that you're any less qualified for the call because you find it challenging to complete. If anything, these are the moments that remind you that even in your weakness, God is strong and His grace is sufficient for all of your needs.

In addition to praying, understand that each season will be different. You may need to shift your priorities for a while, ask for help, or even create a schedule or routine that allows you to manage all you've been tasked with. Some days you may feel like you have it all together, while other days may feel more challenging. But just know that whichever day you're experiencing, God will give you the grace to get through it.

In addition to **praying**, understand that each **season** will be different.

God knows what you can handle, but He also knows all the things you struggle with. He's not surprised when you bring your burdens to Him. In fact, that's what He desires from us. Like I mentioned in chapter 1, God is fully capable (and ready) to answer your questions. The Bible tells us to cast our cares and worries on Him because He cares for us (1 Peter 5:7). And this moment is no different.

CONSIDER

I can do all things through Christ who strengthens me.

Philippians 4:13 NKJV

EXAMINE

What are some things that have been overwhelming you in this season? Do you truly feel that you are in alignment with God's timing, or do you feel like you may be rushing ahead?

....

....

....

....

OFFER

God, I thank You for trusting me with this assignment. Even when the road isn't easy, I am committed to carrying out the call that You have placed on my life. I invite You to come in and readjust anything that is out of order and hindering my progress. I trust that Your timing is the best timing. In Jesus' name, amen.

13

WHAT'S NEXT?

Have you ever been driving a route you've been on a thousand times when you abruptly hit an unexpected detour? Whether it's due to an accident, roadwork, or something else, you suddenly can't take your normal route.

It's happened to me plenty, but the times I remember the most were before smartphones existed. Once on the hour-long commute from my hometown to my college campus, I was forced to take a different route than the one I had memorized. As I drove through a few neighborhoods, the scenery looked less and less familiar, and fear started to creep in. This route wasn't in my original plans. Thankfully, before my thoughts completely spiraled out of control, the detour led me to a place I recognized, and before I knew it,

I had found my way and made it to my destination—and on time too.

I believe the same thing happens to us in life. We get so familiar with how things are going, and the moment we're faced with even the slightest change, we're thrown off. Whether we're forced to pivot on an idea that God placed in our heart or having to switch careers just when we were getting comfortable, change smacks us right in the face. Before we know it we begin to question everything we thought we knew. It's scary to face a new set of plans that we haven't factored into the picture.

But here's what I want you to know: Although the route you take may change, it's fully possible that the *destination* will stay the same.

Sometimes we focus so much on *how* we're going to get there that we forget we're not even the one in the driver's seat. We are simply passengers with God along this journey called *life*, and He is the one leading the way.

Although **the route you take** may change, it's fully possible that the **destination** will stay the same.

Imagine a long and winding road, with hills and valleys, detours, and maybe even a little traffic that slows you down at some points. If the destination is important enough to you, you'll find a way to keep going. It won't matter how long it takes to reach the destination or how many stops you make along the way or how many times you contemplate turning back, because you know there is something waiting for you on the other side of your arrival. The same is true about life and our God-given assignments. The path you take to reach those dreams and goals doesn't always need to be set in stone. There's more than one way to reach your destination. Being flexible can be one of the best things you do.

A **detour** is not the end of the **journey.**

If you ever find yourself feeling overwhelmed about how your path is unfolding, remember this: The more room you leave for the unexpected, the more space God has to move in your life. I know it's easier said than done, but if you can release your need to be in control of your journey, you'll remove some of that unnecessary pressure.

A detour is not the end of the journey.

Nor is a minor setback.

Nor is a complete pivot.

The journey is still the journey. Whether it's what you *planned* for or not.

This may seem counterintuitive, but if everything went according to plan, we'd miss out on opportunities to grow our faith. I'm convinced that the unexpected moments in life are the ones when we experience the most growth. We might not like the challenges and setbacks, but they surely make us stronger.

If everything went **according to plan**, we'd miss out on opportunities to **grow our faith**.

Bottom line? Don't allow the unexpected moments to send you on a downward spiral rooted in fear. Trust me: You will arrive at your destination exactly when you're supposed to. God will make sure of it.

CONSIDER

Trust in the LORD with all your heart and lean not on your own understanding; in all your ways submit to him, and he will make your paths straight.

Proverbs 3:5–6 NIV

EXAMINE

What unforeseen detours have you taken in life when pursuing your goals? How can you shift your perspective and learn to trust God in the process?

....

....

....

OFFER

God, I thank You for directing my path and even for the detours that You put in place to keep me safe on this journey. I know that Your plans are better than my own, and You go to great lengths to make sure I get the best of the best. I ask that You help me to remain flexible in whatever path You call me to pursue. In Jesus' name, amen.

14

HOW DO I CONTINUE THROUGH DISAPPOINTMENT?

After I had our first daughter, Olivia, I was diagnosed with secondary infertility. *Devastated* isn't a word I use often, but this is probably the one time in life when it accurately described how I felt. All my plans had suddenly been tossed out the window. Watching my kids play together while I cooked Saturday morning breakfast? Gone. Being able to grant my daughter's wish of becoming a big sister? Gone. And it felt like there was nothing I could do about it.

During this season of infertility, I tried home remedies

and supplements for a while, but eventually I stopped. The mental load of trying to "fix" myself had become too much to handle. I decided in that moment that I was just going to let go and give it to God. I bought two onesies, put them in my Bible, and left my tears and prayers in the hands of God. Even though I was disappointed with my situation, I believed that God could fix it.

And He did.

Less than two months later, we were expecting again. It's crazy how we can experience disappointment in one season and God can turn it into a full-blown testimony in the next.

Whether we want to admit it or not, disappointment is something each of us experiences. This happens when we have desires, but because of life's circumstances, we may not get the thing that we're hoping and praying for exactly when we want it—or ever.

It's crazy how we can experience **disappointment in one season** and God can turn it into a **full-blown testimony** in the next.

Many of us have a natural instinct to take things into our own hands in an effort to speed up the process. We may even (unintentionally) try to "play God" over our situation. We start brainstorming how we can solve our own problems rather than turning them over to God. No matter how much we try to strategize or how many people we seek advice from, God is the only one who can turn it around. But just because we've been called to wait on God, that doesn't give us a free pass to live in disappointment until He answers our prayer. If anything, these are the moments when we should be leaning into our faith and trusting Him with the outcome even more.

Now isn't the time to give up on **what you're praying for** but rather a time to **be intentional** about how you wait.

Just because you don't get what you want in the moment doesn't mean that you won't *ever* get it. But what you do while you wait matters.

If you've been stuck in a season of waiting, I want to remind you that God doesn't make us wait because He's not going to give us what we've asked for, because a blessing too soon isn't a blessing at all. Perhaps God just wants you to be better prepared before He delivers what you've asked for.

Whether it's making those lifelong dreams come true . . .
Or finally getting your big career break . . .
Or finding success with that creative project you've been working on . . .

Don't let a season of disappointment hijack your joy. For all you know, God is taking this time to expand your capacity so you can handle what's coming your way and be able to steward it well. Now isn't the time to give up on what you're praying for but rather a time to be intentional about how you wait.

Start waiting with a joyful heart.

Start waiting with expectation.

Start waiting with a prayer on your heart that's powerful enough to move mountains.

Start writing down the things that you are trusting God to bring to fruition.

Start living as if it's already happened.

Soon enough, that disappointment will fade away, and not only will you be standing in the middle of everything that God promised you, but you'll have tangible proof of how God showed up—just like He said He would.

Start waiting with a **joyful heart**.

CONSIDER

Wait for the LORD; Be strong and let your heart take courage; Yes, wait for the LORD.

Psalm 27:14 NASB

EXAMINE

What have you been trying to control that can—and should—be released to God? How hard is it for you to trust God's timing?

....

....

....

....

OFFER

God, I pray that You give me the desire to make You my first go-to, not my last resort. I pray that You allow me to bounce back from any disappointment I have experienced in the past and start with a clean slate. I trust Your timing, and I know that whatever You have in store for me won't pass me by. In Jesus' name, amen.

15

WHOSE RACE AM I REALLY RUNNING?

As former athletes, my husband and I were beyond excited when my daughter joined her first official sport—track and field. Wanting her to be prepared, we taught her how to get in her starting stance, how to control her breathing, how to keep her head down until the starter pistol fired, and how to focus on the finish line, not the other runners.

On the day of her first meet, and after we did our family huddle, her coach walked her to the starting line to prepare for her race. When the track official fired the starter pistol, she raced off with the other girls toward the finish line. She did everything we had talked about: head held high, eyes focused on the finish line, and breathing controlled. She was on it. Moments later I heard the announcer say my daughter's name over the loudspeaker. She had come in first place!

When it came time for her second race, she was confident and eager to win again, but as she ran, she looked over and noticed another runner near her, matching her speed. It was in that moment that she lost focus, took her eyes off the finish line, and slowed down with a sense of defeat. Ultimately, taking her eyes off the finish line caused her to lose her place *and* her confidence.

Taking her **eyes off the finish line** caused her to lose her place *and* her **confidence**.

When God gives us an assignment, how often do we start off excited, running full steam ahead, on the right track, and then suddenly we turn our attention to what everyone else is doing around us?

We start internalizing others' progress or success as our own failure, and before long we find ourselves slowing down in our own race, questioning our abilities, unknowingly planting seeds of doubt, and chipping away at our confidence—all because we took our eyes off the mark.

Theodore Roosevelt reportedly said, "Comparison is the thief of joy," and I wholeheartedly agree. Not only will comparison steal your joy, but it'll steal more than that if you let it—like your drive, your hope, your peace, and even your faith if you let it.

So here's what you need to remember while you're pursuing the vision that God has placed in your heart: He is not sending just *one* person to make an impact; He's sending a multitude to cover every corner of every kingdom assignment. What does that mean for you? It's your duty to take up space in the place where He has called you to serve—and to do it without falling into the Enemy's trap of comparison. The Enemy knows that if he can stop *you*, he can stop the people that are *connected* to you. And if he can stop the people *connected* to you, he can stop the people connected to *them*. I don't know about you, but that gives me even more fuel to stay focused on my own individual assignment.

Your **gifts** are needed.

Just in case you need to hear it again: Your gifts are needed. So are your ideas. So is your story. So is your voice. Don't allow comparison to be the roadblock that stops you from doing what you were created to do.

I know it may not always feel like it, but unlike in sports, there is no single winner in life. We're all put here to run our race and do our part.

Here's what I'm challenging you with: Focus on the finish line.

But even while you're running your own race, encourage those *behind* you who are still trying to find their way. Lock arms with those *beside* you who are working diligently toward their own God-given assignments. And cheer for those *ahead* of you who have found their way and are making a positive impact for the kingdom.

When one wins, **we all win**.

We are all racing toward the same finish line: to be good stewards of everything that God has entrusted us with. When one wins, we all win.

CONSIDER

Let your eyes look directly forward, and your gaze be straight before you.

Proverbs 4:25 ESV

EXAMINE

In what ways has comparison impacted the way you show up? How can you shift your focus and regain your excitement about what God has called you to pursue?

....

....

....

....

....

OFFER

God, I know You have given each of us a unique gift and purpose. Help me to stay focused on my own. I ask that You remove any feelings of comparison so that I can cheer others on and not internalize their success as my failure. In Jesus' name, amen.

16

WHAT IF IT ALL WORKS OUT?

It was the first official date that I had planned for my boyfriend (now husband) and me, and I wanted to prove to him that I could be fun and adventurous. I wasn't shy with taking a risk or two, but in this particular instance, I might have bitten off more than I could chew: I had signed us up for a zip-lining adventure. It wasn't until we got to the park that I realized all the date entailed. Not only would we be zip-lining, but the reservation also included treetop adventures, free falls, a ropes course, and more.

We completed the majority of the course, but the free fall into a net nearly took me out. The drop in my stomach was a feeling I still remember to this day. I was ready to get the date over with, but before we headed toward the exit, the instructor asked if we wanted to take the zip line back since it would be quicker. We agreed and followed along to the next stop. As we climbed the tree, I noticed just how high up we were going, and with each step, I regretted my decision.

I had no other option but to close my eyes, **trust God**, and *literally* **take the leap**.

As we reached the very top and I saw the view, I instantly attempted to turn around and head back. The problem was that there was now a line of anxious adventurers waiting behind us and the instructor told us, "No turning back." *Worried* isn't the word I'd use to describe how I felt. I was *terrified*. At this point, I had no other option but to close my eyes, trust God, and *literally* take the leap. Turns out the ride wasn't that bad, and I made it safely to the bottom. *Whew!* "Thank God for His traveling mercies" took on a whole new meaning for me.

How often does this happen in our day-to-day lives, especially when we have an expectation of how something will go? The moment we realize that things are going in a different direction, worry can begin to consume our thoughts. For some reason, when our plans or desires don't unfold in the way we had anticipated, we allow our feathers to get ruffled.

Our timeline is not always in alignment with **God's plans**.

Is it valid to have desires and plans for how you envision things to unfold? Yes. In fact, the Bible tells us that when we delight ourselves in the Lord, He will give us the desires of our heart (Psalm 37:4). The problem isn't the desire itself; it's when we become attached to one way of doing things or to a specific timeline.

You're praying for the opportunities, but you want them right now.

You're praying for the increase in finances, but you want it right now.

You're praying for the idea to be a success, but you want it right now.

When we put time (or any) restrictions on when and how we expect God to act, we begin to worry while we wait. A hard truth that I've learned over the years is that our timeline (or the way we envision things unfolding) is not always in alignment with *God's* plans. That doesn't mean we won't get what we're asking for; it simply means that God's timing is better than ours and maybe we'll get it when the time is right.

One thing about God is that He always keeps His promises and everything will happen exactly at the right time. You don't have to live in a state of worry while you wait. You can choose to have faith and trust that whatever God has in store for you will reach you when the time is right—even if that means closing your eyes and taking those big scary leaps of faith. If you're showing up, doing your part, and meeting God where you are, that's more than enough. Your journey will lead you exactly where you're supposed to be.

Your **journey** will lead you exactly where you're **supposed to be**.

CONSIDER

We can make our plans, but the LORD determines our steps.

Proverbs 16:9 NLT

EXAMINE

Can you remember a time when God came through for you at the eleventh hour? What made you anxious then and how did that turn out? What is making you anxious right now? How can you turn it over to God?

....

....

....

OFFER

God, I pray that You remove any anxiousness that is hindering me from pursuing what You've called me to do. I ask that You help me to remember that Your timing is better than anything I could ever plan on my own. I thank You for a calm spirit, a peaceful mind, and a patient heart. I trust that the blessings You have in store for me are already in motion and will arrive exactly when they're supposed to. In Jesus' name, amen.

17

HOW DO I HOLD ON TO HOPE?

I landed my first official "big girl" job just a few months out of college. I attended company training sessions and met with team members in leadership roles, and I just knew this was it: my big career break. That was my start in climbing the corporate ladder—or so I thought!

It wasn't until I'd been on the job for a few months that I realized the day-to-day work was unfulfilling. I was thankful for the income, but I knew there was something missing. I showed up day after day and performed daily tasks I had little to no interest in, all while forcing myself to smile so I would be considered a team player. As the days passed I became more and more hopeless about my future. It became harder to convince myself that I had "made it."

I thought the journey would be easier—a lot easier. I kept those feelings to myself for a while and went through the motions, but eventually I realized this hopeless feeling was not only stripping me of my joy, but was also dimming my fire. It was a struggle, but I knew I had to fight to get my ambition and hope back. I always say, "It's a good thing that you only need faith the size of a mustard seed," because that's all I had in that moment. Turns out it was more than enough.

You still have to **show up**.

If you ever feel like you're losing your fire and becoming hopeless, I want you to remember that pursuing your purpose won't always be easy. When you're pursuing something you've never done before, you may encounter some of your most challenging moments. And unless God has given you a specific time frame, there's no way for you to know when His promises will come to fruition or what the journey to get there will look like. Yet you still have to show up. For most of us, that can be challenging.

Following the dream but waiting for the reward.

Saying the prayers but waiting for an answer.

Showing up when quitting seems easier.

What do you do while you wait? How do you stay optimistic? How do you continue to show up even when you're feeling hopeless?

This may sound cliché, but you must remember your *why*. What were your thoughts and emotions when you were at your highest? Keep that at the forefront of your mind as often as possible. Then take inventory of why you're feeling hopeless or defeated. Is there something you can change? Or is it something you need to release to God? Remember when I mentioned having faith the size of a mustard seed? Find that faith and hold on to it as tightly as you can. Allow 2 Corinthians 5:7 to be your daily guide: "We live by faith, not by sight" (NIV). What you see may not be what was asked for, but that doesn't mean it's not on the way. You could be mid-miracle and not even know it.

You must **remember your why**.

Although we only see things from our point of view, there are so many other aspects and details that God is working on behind the scenes, and we can be sure that He is not passing out rushed, half-baked blessings. When He delivers, those blessings will be complete.

You may not know when it will happen, but you cannot afford to lose your hope while you wait. That's exactly what the Enemy is counting on. Because the sooner you quit, the less of a threat you are. He knows that if you stick it out and get to the other side of the struggle, not only will *your* life be forever changed, but the people you are called to serve—their lives will be changed too.

Feelings of hopeless won't last **forever**.

Feelings of hopelessness won't last forever. Learn to quickly recognize when those feelings creep in, and do whatever you can to pull yourself out. Don't become complacent, mired in hopelessness. What God has promised you will be well worth the wait.

CONSIDER

Don't worry about anything; instead, pray about everything. Tell God what you need, and thank him for all he has done.

Philippians 4:6 NLT

EXAMINE

Can you recall a time when you felt hopeless but everything ended up working out for your good? How can you choose to be optimistic about your future today?

....

....

....

....

....

OFFER

God, I pray You will help me remain hopeful during the wait. I know that there are miracles headed my way, and I fully trust You with my future. I know that my best days are ahead of me. In Jesus' name, amen.

18

AM I BLOCKING MY BLESSINGS?

Before I started my business, Christian Entrepreneur Organization (CEO), I had already tried almost a dozen other passion projects (aka "failed business ventures"). So by the time I was ready to launch CEO, I had an overwhelming sense of embarrassment when it came to launching yet *another* business.

If I'm being completely honest, it wasn't that I was afraid of failing; I was afraid of people *seeing* me fail (again). If they already knew my last ventures had failed, why would they bother supporting this one? What would make people believe that I knew what I was doing this time? How could I convince them that I was an expert?

While I felt both excited and nervous to start a new venture, I found myself focusing so much on what other people might say that I began to lose sight of the very thing God had called me to do. And even though I knew this time was different, I still let embarrassment impact how I showed up—being secretive about what I was pursuing, shying away from any conversation revolving around business, and keeping my dreams hidden away in my notebook in the back of my nightstand. I wasn't ready to publicly declare my ambitions again.

> It's clear to see that even though my prior **passion projects** hadn't been a hit, they still **played a major part** in where I am today.

In hindsight, it's clear to see that even though my prior passion projects hadn't been a hit, they still played a major part in where I am today. It didn't seem like it in the moment, but each failed venture had led me to this moment—and to building something bigger than I ever could've imagined. Ten years ago I had no idea that I'd be impacting hundreds of thousands of women, or shipping products all over the world, or even coaching women to launch their own businesses, but seeing how God has orchestrated everything to come full circle has been nothing short of amazing.

It doesn't matter what it *feels* like, it's always in your best interest to give yourself grace as you explore new territories. Everyone starts out as a beginner, even the best of the best. And truthfully, it's a bit naive for us to pursue new things and expect to face zero challenges along the way. I mean, it *sounds* nice to have all the puzzle pieces to easily fall into place, but in theory, not encountering any challenges would rob us of the opportunity to gain experience and learn something new.

Some **assignments** are simply a **stepping stone** to get you where you're ultimately supposed to be.

Here's a hard but necessary truth: Not every idea or vision will result in financial success. I know that might be a hard pill to swallow, but God isn't concerned only with your ability to live financially free. He also wants you to have the right heart posture to reveal your strengths and weaknesses so you can show up as your best self, and He wants to get you to a point of unwavering faith that you move when He speaks, without hesitation.

Some assignments are simply a stepping stone to get you where you're ultimately supposed to be. Step one prepares you for step two, step two prepares you for step three, and so on. But if you're not willing to take the first step, you'll never get to the intended destination.

Not only are you **called**, you're **equipped**.

Be open to trying new things and let go of the belief that everything needs to be perfect, because more than likely, there will be some missteps. As I mentioned before, God is not looking for perfection; He's looking for obedience.

He's looking for you to show up.

He's looking for you to follow His voice.

He's looking for you to take notice of any distractions that impact your forward movement.

He's looking for you to take action and build momentum for the vision He has placed in your heart.

Regardless of how you feel or how you think others will perceive you, you must keep moving forward. Yes, you'll make mistakes. Yes, you may feel apprehensive about continuing to put yourself out there. But don't let what you *feel* get in the way of what you *know*.

Not only are you called, you're equipped.

CONSIDER

"Forget about what's happened; don't keep going over old history. Be alert, be present. I'm about to do something brand-new."

Isaiah 43:18–19 MSG

EXAMINE

What past failures or disappointments have you been embarrassed about? How is your relationship to those failures hindering the way you show up today?

....

....

....

OFFER

God, help me to keep my focus on You while I am pursuing what You have placed in my heart. Help me to not be distracted by the opinions of others and to give myself grace while navigating this new territory. I trust that You are lining up the pieces of my life perfectly and that You are preparing me for what's ahead. In Jesus' name, amen.

19

IS PRIDE HOLDING ME BACK?

Years ago, before I knew anything about purpose, I was naively under the impression that my gifts and talents were things I had acquired on my own. I spent a lot of time trying to find creative ways to use my gifts, only for them to work halfway. I had always reserved conversations with God for the other areas of my life: family, safety, daily problems—those sorts of things. I had never thought to include Him in the pursuit of my dreams. As far as I was concerned, that was something I could accomplish on my own.

Pride.

That's what it was, plain and simple. And here's the kicker: Nothing truly took off for me until I invited God in. Clearly *my* efforts alone were not enough. It wasn't until I was in alignment with what God wanted for me that I started to gain any traction.

Nothing truly took off for me until I **invited God in**.

Sometimes we don't want to "bother" God with the seemingly small things (which is impossible, by the way), but other times, it's simply because of our pride. When we are operating from a place of pride, we shut God out. We think we can accomplish the task on our own, and it's not until we hit rock bottom that we invite God in. Some of us treat our relationship with God as if we're on the TV show *Who Wants to Be a Millionaire*—and we have only *one* lifeline call. We tend to put God on a shelf until we *really* need Him—not on "small" things like pursuing our dreams; we'd rather try to figure that out on our own.

But here's what I've learned: It doesn't matter how gifted, talented, or passionate you are. If you don't partner with God, you will never walk in your full potential. You will forever find yourself starting and stopping because you are operating in your own strength instead of allowing Him in and operating with His. I'm sure you've heard it before, but God truly does want to be included in every detail of your life.

Lay down the idea that you can (or must) do this alone, because you don't—and you shouldn't. Once you realize this you'll understand how much better the experience will be when you partner with God.

Maybe you're wondering, *Well, how do I do that?* Thankfully, there's more than one way to invite God into your plans. And speaking of *your* plans, the first step is to surrender your own personal ambitions to make sure you are in alignment with God's desires for you. Whatever that is might not be what's popular or what you had envisioned for yourself, but a key part of partnering with God is allowing Him to lead the way.

Next you need to surrender the outcome to God. It's easy to get stuck in your head with how you want things to play out, but as I've mentioned before, when you truly let God lead the way, you need to be open to the unexpected. After all, He knows the best path for you and in what ways you can operate at your full potential.

Some things can't be self-taught or learned through

> Don't allow **pride** to keep you stuck in the same **cycles**.

a course or even from a coach or mentor. Some strategies and creative directions will come only when you invite God into what you're doing—not just asking Him to be a part of *your* plans but making sure you are in alignment with His.

All in all, don't allow pride to keep you stuck in the same cycles year after year.

If you're lacking self-confidence, take it to God.

If you need more clarity on how to move forward, take it to God.

If you feel like you're lacking creativity, take it to God.

I don't care how much you think you can achieve on your own, you always need God's guidance. If you want to do something right, do it with God.

CONSIDER

When pride comes, then comes disgrace, but with the humble is wisdom.

Proverbs 11:2 ESV

EXAMINE

When it comes to pursuing your dreams, do you feel that you've been prideful or resistant to inviting God in? How has this impacted your progress?

....

....

....

....

OFFER

God, I pray that You will restore me where I have been prideful. I don't ever want to lose sight of the fact that I need You in every area of my life. I thank You for every gift and idea that You have called me to pursue, and I pray that You get the glory in all that I do. In Jesus' name, amen.

20

AM I HONORING MY GIFTS?

My children are in this phase where it seems like they're always asking for something. My eldest daughter's latest obsession is jewelry making. Meanwhile my youngest is into any and everything. Whether it's a bead set or a new toy, if she sees it, she wants it. To make sure that our girls don't grow up to be entitled adults, my husband and I continuously do gratitude practices with them.

"You want a new toy? Have you played with the ones that you already have? You want a new bead kit? Have you used the ones you already have? You want new crafting supplies? Have you made use of what we already have?" We're not trying to avoid buying them new things altogether, but we want to make sure they know how to be resourceful and use what's already in their possession.

This is a good practice for children, but it's also a great practice for adults too. How often do we find ourselves asking God for more without even acknowledging what's already in our hands? We're constantly looking for the next best thing, even if we're already living in the middle of an answered prayer. Whether we're looking for more resources, more money, more ideas, more opportunities, or more relationships, we find ourselves coming back to God for more when we haven't even taken inventory of all that He's already given us.

How often do we find ourselves **asking God for more** without even acknowledging what's **already in our hands**?

Maybe we do this out of habit because we've been conditioned to always be in pursuit of *more*. We don't even realize we're doing it. To avoid becoming complacent, we should be mindful and come to God as good stewards of what He's already entrusted us with.

Are you giving your corporate job 100 percent effort while also praying to become a full-time entrepreneur?

Are you taking good care of your ten-year-old car while

still dreaming of driving the latest model to hit the showroom floor?

Are you managing your existing finances well while praying for increase?

Are you using your gifts for your small audience while dreaming of reaching the masses?

Are you being a good steward of the things that you *already* have?

This reminds me of the parable of the talents (Matthew 25:14–30) in which the master gives three of his servants a specified number of talents to manage while he is away on a trip. To the first he gives five talents, to the second he gives two, and to the third he gives one. When the master returns, he finds that only the first two servants did something with their talents and had an increase to offer, while the third servant did nothing but bury his to keep it safe, and returned it in its original state.

How many times do we unintentionally do this to God? We bury the gifts and ideas that He puts in our heart while we wait for more, not knowing that we have the ability to *create* more. You see, it's one thing for God to give us the blessing, but it's another thing for us to take it, be a good steward of it, and increase it.

Being a good steward of your gifts and ideas might

mean taking the words that God has placed in your heart and writing them down even though you don't know how they'll be used. It could also mean pursuing the ministry even though you don't know all the details. It might even mean following His instructions to launch a business even though you don't have all the resources. Being a good steward means being obedient with the resources that God gives you, regardless of how you perceive your current situation. It's truly an act of faith over fear.

Gratitude doesn't mean that God gives you everything you've asked for; it means you're going to make the most of what's **already in your hands**.

You may not have everything you think you need, but surely there's something you can produce out of what you *do* have. Gratitude doesn't mean that God gives you everything you've asked for; it means you're going to make the most of what's already in your hands.

Be grateful and resourceful. No matter what season you're in, all you have is all you need.

CONSIDER

Give thanks in all circumstances; for this is the will of God in Christ Jesus for you.

1 Thessalonians 5:18 ESV

EXAMINE

Reflect on your resources of time, finances, and knowledge. Can you confidently say that you are putting to use what you already have? If not, explain.

....

....

....

....

....

OFFER

God, I ask that You help me to be mindful of everything You have already given me. Help me to be resourceful and use what I have while I wait for what's to come. I trust that all I have is all I need. In Jesus' name, amen.

21

HAVE I PLANNED FOR SUCCESS?

Lately I've been in my Pinterest era. I find tons of recipes that I want to make for my family. Whether it's savory meals, a homemade version of our favorite snacks, or a new side dish, I have a board full of ideas.

Normally when I'm in the kitchen, I'm an "eyeball it to measure it" type of girl. It's not often that I pull out a measuring cup. I remember making my first batch of homemade cookies. I gathered all the ingredients, preheated the oven, skimmed through the instructions, and got to work. While I did measure everything, I completely skipped the step-by-step instructions. In other words, I was convinced that the order wasn't as important as the ingredients—and I was completely wrong.

As the cookies cooled and we had our first taste test, the flavor wasn't what we thought it would be, and they were also completely flat—not fluffy like the picture in the original recipe. Skipping ahead had cost me the quality of the outcome. Had I been just a little more patient and read the entire recipe, I would've nailed it. So that's exactly what I did the next time. Determined to get those cookies as close to perfect as I could, in my next attempt I followed the instructions exactly, and I made the best cookies I had ever made.

It's not enough to just get the assignment from God. You have to stick with Him throughout the process. Whether you're writing a book, pursuing a new idea, or even making a career move, it's always going to be in your best interest to stay close to God from start to finish.

It's always going to be in your **best** interest to **stay close to God** from start to finish.

When God gives you a vision and a plan for how to execute it, you're much more likely to see it through if you stay connected to Him during the process. That's not because the challenges miraculously stop. It's because the God of heaven is backing you and will make sure you succeed.

And because of this, you're better prepared to handle whatever life throws your way.

As we grow older, we tend to expect things to be difficult. But sometimes it's because *we* are the ones making them more difficult. And sometimes it's because we're just flat-out rushing and skipping ahead. Other times it's because we've taken on a mindset of defeat. Whether it's the result of past failures or just feeling weighed down by all that comes with life, we sometimes reach a point where we begin bracing ourselves for disappointment. But here's my question to you: What if you took life's setbacks and still moved forward with a can-do attitude? And what if whenever *you* "messed up," you gave yourself another shot at getting it right instead of accepting defeat?

As the saying goes, "If you fail to plan, you're planning to fail." So, creating a plan of action is key if you want to keep yourself on track with all that God has tasked you with. Start by following His directions *without* attempting to skip ahead. That might look like mapping out your end goal and breaking it down into smaller, more achievable goals to keep you on track. To do this you need to have some idea of what God is calling you to do. What impact is He calling you to make? Who is He calling you to serve? Once you can pinpoint the *what* and the *who*, you can move on to the *how*. Sometimes it's as simple as having quiet time with the Lord with a journal and pen nearby to write down whatever He puts on your heart. This will help you keep a running log of what direction He wants you to take.

Another thing you might find helpful is to identify your weaknesses so you can recognize when you're near the point of quitting. The sooner you can become aware of this and get in front of things, the more you can redirect your energy. You can also create a routine that allows you to show up consistently but without working yourself to the point of burnout. You might also consider keeping a vision board that reminds you of your why and offers you a real-time view of what you're working toward.

The sooner you can **get in front of things**, the more you can **redirect your energy**.

Overall, feeling determined isn't something that just happens; it's something you plan for, something you are intentional about. As long as you have a plan, stay close to God, and are persistent, there is nothing that can stop you from achieving the vision God has put in your heart.

CONSIDER

For you have need of endurance, so that when you have done the will of God you may receive what is promised.

Hebrews 10:36 ESV

EXAMINE

Have you been persistent in pursuing the things that God has called you to do? If not, what's stopping you?

....

....

....

....

OFFER

God, I pray that You increase my determination and my focus. Give me the strength to push past any distractions so I can finish the work You've called me to do. If challenges should arise, I pray You help me remember that You have already gone before me in making sure I am successful with all that You've entrusted me to do. In Jesus' name, amen.

22

HOW DO I QUIET THE NOISE?

It was 11:30 p.m. when I arrived at the hospital ready to deliver my second child. Because I already had one delivery under my belt, I knew without a doubt that I was in active labor. The only problem was the labor and delivery staff didn't think I was dilated enough, so their first response was to send me home to wait it out. They made all kinds of suggestions, everything from walking laps around the house to stretching on a yoga ball to breathing deeply through the contractions. They even suggested that I try to get some rest. (Yeah, right!)

Two hours passed, and I suddenly knew it was time to push, even though I was still being told I wasn't dilated enough. I made my way to the bed just as my doctor arrived. And what do you know—it *was* time to push. But now it was too late to receive any pain medication. There was no turning back. Approximately ten minutes and a few short pushes later, our youngest daughter, Sydney, was born—despite the hospital staff's belief that I wasn't close to delivering.

There are times in our lives when we know without a doubt that it's time for the next phase, even if the people around us don't quite believe it yet. They might offer other options because they don't truly understand our position. They don't know what God has spoken to us. They don't know how long we've labored, and they don't fully understand the vision. So instead of taking our word for it, they offer unsolicited (and often unhelpful) advice.

There are **times in our lives** when we know without a doubt that it's **time for the next phase**, even if the people around us don't quite believe it yet.

"If I were you, I'd try something else."

"There are already too many people doing that. The market is already saturated."

"What if it doesn't work?"

But here's the thing: When it's time to push, it's time to

push. And you'll know it, whether it's time for pursuing a new idea, stepping up to serve in ministry, taking on a mentorship role, or even making lifestyle changes related to your overall health and wellness. When it's time to go to the next level, God will let you know. And because of this you must be mindful of the conversations you engage in.

Why? Because it's not uncommon for people to project their own fears onto you. Whether people do this intentionally or not, you can't allow those opinions to make you second-guess the very thing that God has already confirmed for you.

Even though people won't always agree with (or understand) the moves you're setting yourself up to make, you must trust the conversations that you have with God over the ones you have with your peers. They may mean well, but outside approval is not a prerequisite for doing what God is calling you to.

Outside approval is not a prerequisite for doing **what God is calling** you to.

These are the moments when you truly get the opportunity to exercise your faith. I had no intention of giving birth without an epidural that night. The thought hadn't even crossed my mind. But in that moment I had to trust God and push anyway, despite what the people around me were saying or how I was feeling. When it's go time, it's go time.

No matter how uncomfortable your circumstances may be, you need to believe without a doubt that you are capable of doing whatever God calls you to do. That's not to say you won't feel apprehensive when it's time to step into the next phase, but please understand that that's not an indicator that you're incapable of moving forward. Sure, you might be stepping into unfamiliar territory, but you can make your way through by relying on the conversations between you and God instead of seeking outside validation. You must be sure of it for *yourself*.

When you get in the habit of seeking agreement or approval from others, you subconsciously train your mind that their approval is a necessity. But what happens when God tells you to do something that others don't agree with? Or something that goes against the grain of the masses? How will you respond? This is why it's important to quiet any outside voices or noise so you can hear God's voice loud and clear.

And remember, even if no one else can see the vision, your job is to show up with confidence and pursue it anyway.

CONSIDER

Jesus looked at them and said, "With man it is impossible, but not with God. For all things are possible with God."

Mark 10:27 ESV

EXAMINE

What has God been pushing you to do that you've been hesitant about? How have you allowed the opinions of others to get in the way of your obedience?

....

....

....

OFFER

God, I know that people mean well when offering advice, but I pray that You will remind me of the conversations You and I have had and let those outweigh anything that tries to deter me from showing up. I believe that You know what's best for me and that You will guide my steps in the direction they should go. In Jesus' name, amen.

PART 3 WRAP-UP

ACTION PLAN TO IDENTIFY HOMEGROWN HURDLES

It's been a while since our last check-in, so let's pause here. I want to make sure we're still moving in the right direction. In this last part, we covered a ton of information—everything from imposter syndrome and comparison to pride, fear, and more. These emotions are a natural human response to life's experiences. We may not always be able to avoid them, but if we can learn how to manage them, we'll be that much better off.

Take some time to work through the following action steps.

STEP #1: WHAT EMOTIONS DO YOU STRUGGLE WITH MOST? CAN YOU IDENTIFY WHAT TRIGGERS THEM?

Which emotions from this section are coming up most often for you? Make note of what triggers those feelings. Is there a pattern for when certain emotions arise? Once you can identify this, you'll have a better understanding of what to do (or stop doing) to reduce the frequency of those feelings.

STEP #2: WHAT BOUNDARIES CAN YOU CREATE FOR YOURSELF TO HELP MANAGE YOUR EMOTIONS?

Looking back at action step number 1, can you recognize repeated emotions? Do you know what makes you feel anxious, what makes you feel fearful, or even what frustrates you?

Having personal boundaries in place—whether with people, places, or things—will help you choose better responses to those feelings when they arise.

STEP #3: SCHEDULE MOMENTS FOR REST.

Whether weekly or biweekly, give your body and mind enough time to rest. Pursuing those ideas that God has placed on your heart is not a substitute for rest, and you don't need to spend every ounce of your free time proving your obedience. He already sees it.

PART 4

FIND THE COURAGE TO MOVE FORWARD

EMBRACE THE UNKNOWN AND TRUST GOD'S PLAN

We often hear the admonition to "have courage," but what does that *actually* mean? Is it the act of being fearless? Is it believing that you're capable of achieving the impossible? Is it being bold and brave in the face of adversity? According to the dictionary, *courage* means having the "mental or moral strength to venture, persevere, and withstand danger, fear, or difficulty"—essentially, doing something that frightens you.

Courage is something we all aspire to have, but ironically, it's probably one of the most challenging qualities to embody—it takes courage to be courageous. Stepping into unknown territory and not knowing what lies ahead is incredibly challenging, more than we'd care to admit. But gaining courage is similar to building a muscle—the more we do it, the stronger we get. And just like building muscle, growing courage doesn't typically happen overnight.

In this final section we'll focus on how to build courage. Your work and purpose aren't done when you finish reading this book. In fact, your journey is just beginning as you start to put what you've learned into practice in real life. No matter what God is calling you to do, obedience and courage will keep you moving forward. Whether that means taking more risks, embracing failure along the way, or even transforming your mind to believe in the impossible, courage is a core part of how you show up.

23

ADMIT THAT YOU NEED HELP

A few years ago God gave me the vision of hosting my first in-person event, and as a person who enjoys being behind the scenes, I really wasn't too keen on the idea. I mean, I barely felt comfortable showing my face *online*—how on earth was I supposed to lead an entire event *in person*?

I put it off for a while, but eventually those gentle nudges became firm taps. When I realized I couldn't escape this calling, I gave God my yes—even if it seemed quiet and unsure.

I began planning the logistics of everything, and then just like clockwork, fear set in. *How are you going to plan this with no team? How will you sell tickets? Maybe you should get a smaller venue just in case you can't fill it. What if you have to cancel?*

I was scared, but I didn't back down. I launched the tickets, prayed for the best, and within two weeks, we sold out. Twice. I went from thinking, *Who's really going to come to this event?* to, *Wow, I should've looked for a bigger venue.*

Everything I had been worried about, God already had under control. When God calls you to pursue something, He'll send everything you need to make it happen, including support. Where most of us get stuck is needing to know the who, what, when, where, why, and how *before* we're willing to make a move. It's almost as if we're saying to God, "Prove it first, *then* I'll do it."

Everything I had been worried about, **God already had under control**.

Spoiler alert: God already has a proven track record. At some point, you just have to take Him at His word. You have to trust that not only does He know what you need, but He also knows when to deliver it. Wanting to be supported in the things that God is calling you to do is normal. That's what most of us want. However, if that's a requirement for your obedience, I have to tell you, you're missing out.

Here's why: Some seasons will be just for you and God—to increase your faith, to learn how to hear His voice, to trust that He knows best. And if you're breezing past those seasons because you're rushing to the next one, you might not see all the good that's happening right in front of you.

Additionally, what you're *expecting* and what God actually *sends* might look a lot different.

You may be expecting family and friends to be your main sources of support, but what God really has for you is a group of strangers lined up, waiting to lock arms with you to move your vision forward. God knows exactly the people you need in your corner, and sometimes it's those you least expect. Be open to receiving support from people beyond your inner circle. You never know who God has in place to help elevate your calling.

God knows exactly the **people you need** in your corner, and sometimes it's **those you least expect**.

You may think your gifts can't go beyond your local community, while God is actually putting your name in rooms that you know nothing about—dropping your name into the hearts of people who are able to help you get to the next level. You never know what types of resources or connections will come simply because of your obedience.

You might be expecting to run into certain challenges, but He has already ironed out the details and has gone before you to make sure things work out for your good. The stumbling blocks that would normally take others out will teach you lessons that ultimately move you one step closer to your vision.

The thing about God is that He's always several steps ahead of us. He knows what we need and also when we need to release something. Think of it this way: Consider how marathons have aid stations set up throughout a course with water, healthy snacks, or first-aid supplies. These checkpoints are in place to support the runners on their journey. And guess what? Runners don't have to go out of their way to find them. The marathon organizers plan in advance so the runners have whatever they need as they race toward the finish line.

The same is true for us. When we are obedient in doing what God calls us to do, we don't have to worry about where the support or resources will come from. It's already handled. God has already gone before you and set people in place to help you move the vision forward. Your job is to keep running.

CONSIDER

And we know that for those who love God all things work together for good, for those who are called according to his purpose.

Romans 8:28 ESV

EXAMINE

Do you feel like you are lacking support in any areas? How does that impact the way you show up?

....

....

....

....

OFFER

God, I thank You for each season on this journey. Even when it's a season where it's just the two of us, I trust that my every need will be met. I pray that You will not let my heart become hardened and that it remains soft and open, ready to receive anyone You send to help me move this vision forward. In Jesus' name, amen.

24

CHECK THE MANUAL

"I'm returning this."

My husband and I had the bright idea to make homemade veggie fried rice and chicken on our Blackstone griddle and had purchased a rice cooker as well, hoping to speed up the process. I unpackaged and washed the rice cooker, not bothering to read the manual since I had already taken a quick glance at the steps listed on the outside of the box. I mean, how hard could it be?

Twenty minutes or so after putting the rice in, I checked it, only to discover that it hadn't even started cooking. I pushed a few more buttons, and ten minutes later, still nothing. Finally I pulled out the instruction manual, followed the steps, and what do you know—it worked, exactly like it was supposed to.

As I sat there shaking my head and laughing at myself and my tendency to think I already know, God stepped in and made it a teachable moment. We often do the same thing with the gifts and ideas that we receive from Him. God places these big ideas on our hearts, we have our light bulb moment of how we think we're going to make them work, and immediately we take off running—sometimes without even asking any follow-up questions.

Is it really **obedience** if we're leaving God out of the process?

We create the business name, register the LLC, launch the website, and purchase the inventory, all before we even have clear instructions on what our next steps are. Then we end up tired, burned-out, and disappointed when things don't work out as we planned—all because we failed to go back and read the manual (aka check in with God).

I get it. We all want to be obedient, but is it really obedience if we're leaving God out of the process? Is it really obedience when we've taken half of His instructions and merged them with half of our own?

There's a reason we call something a "God-given gift" or

a "God-given idea"—because it comes directly from God, and we can't take an opportunity from God and pursue it to its full capacity without Him.

Sure, we might find *some* success going after something on our own, but if we truly want to see that thing flourish to its full potential, we need to invite God to be a part of the process, from start to finish. Instead of allowing those ideas to pull us away from God, we need to let them to push us closer to Him.

We need to **invite God** to be a part of the process.

You're probably wondering, *Well, what does that even look like?*

It looks like being intentional with your prayers, asking God before you make any decisions, praying for the wisdom to know when to move and when to be still, and reading God's Word to help you seek wisdom.

Believe it or not, God has the exact plan to help you find success in what He's calling you to do. But if you never go back to the manual, you may very well be working harder than you need to.

When we try to do things on our own, we end up missing some of the most important parts of the journey. Or even worse, we quit altogether.

I realize that pursuing your dreams is a lot different than

my initial failed attempts at using my rice cooker, but hopefully you can see how the same lesson still applies. When in doubt (and even when you're not), check with God. Not only will it save you time and frustration, but you'll also get the clarity and courage you need to move forward.

Getting off track is one thing, but choosing to *stay* off track is another. It's better to pause for more clarity, do a hard reset if needed, and even go back and read the manual than it is to move forward without God's guidance.

> **Getting off track** is one thing, but **choosing to stay** off track is another.

Whether it be for a rice cooker, a new recipe, or pursuing your gifts and ideas, there is a purpose for a manual. It's not for decoration, nor is it something that's included just because. The manual is there to offer you instructions on how to do something correctly and to its full potential. If you want to work smarter, not harder, stick with God from start to finish.

CONSIDER

"For I know the plans I have for you," declares the LORD, "plans to prosper you and not to harm you, plans to give you hope and a future."

Jeremiah 29:11 NIV

EXAMINE

What ideas has God placed in your heart, but somewhere along the line you've removed Him from the decision-making process? What are two ways you can ensure that you keep God involved?

....

....

....

OFFER

God, I pray that You give me the desire and the wisdom to keep You involved from start to finish. I pray that You help me to slow down when I'm moving too far ahead without You and to speed up if I'm ever too far behind. I don't want to miss Your instructions. Whether it's ego or being naive, please remove any barriers that are causing me not to operate within my full potential. In Jesus' name, amen.

25

WATCH YOUR WORDS

Before I launched my current business, I went through quite a few rough patches. Not knowing what my purpose was, coupled with giving up on my childhood dreams, really did a number on me. I had always dreamed of using my creativity to build something that would outlive me, perhaps a huge corporation that would not only make my family proud but also change the trajectory of our lives.

My dad often told me I could become whatever I wanted to be in life, but the older I got and the more hardships I experienced, the less I believed it. I had lost all hope. I was sure that I had reached my peak in life and there was nothing left to achieve. Some days I'd be able to hide the disappointment I was feeling, but other days I simply couldn't. I would wake up in a funk, uninterested in what the day had to offer, and my irritation was reflected all over my face.

I started **believing** I was **worthy**.

At the time my daughter Olivia was about two years old, I knew I couldn't continue to carry this weight around with me and still show up at my best for her, so I decided to change things up a bit. I took a stack of sticky notes, wrote positive affirmations based on biblical truths on each one, and placed them all over my home.

"I am worthy."

"God has a plan for my life."

"I am capable of doing whatever God calls me to do."

"I am more than enough."

"My breakthrough is coming."

I'm not going to lie—the first few days were tough. Although I was reading the affirmations, I didn't actually *believe* them to be true. I mean, imagine waking up with no excitement about the future and still having to recite "God has a plan for my life." I felt silly.

But as the days went on, I realized that something was changing. Not only did I start looking forward to finding these sticky notes around the house (as if I didn't hide them myself!), but I actually started *believing* what I was saying.

I started believing I was worthy.

I started believing I was capable.

I started believing good things were coming.

And before I knew it my entire thinking about the future had shifted. Not only did my thoughts shift, but so did my reality.

For this reason alone I will forever be an advocate of positive affirmations. And not just any affirmations but those deeply rooted in God's Word, affirmations that point you back to Scripture and remind you of what God says about you.

If you want to change the way you speak about yourself and your future, it's going to take some intentionality. It might not feel natural in the beginning, but the more you do it, the easier it'll become. You might have to start off creating a morning routine with biblical affirmations to help you jump-start your day or keep a notebook nearby to jot down all the gentle reminders that God places on your heart as you go. It might

The key here is to **be intentional with the words** that you are speaking over your life—**no matter what** your current situation looks like.

even be worth your while to create a nighttime routine to help you end your day on a positive note. The key here is to be intentional with the words that you are speaking over your life—no matter what your current situation looks like. Stay hopeful and choose your words wisely. The impact that your words have on your life is bigger than you know.

The **impact** that your **words** have on your **life** is bigger than you know.

CONSIDER

Words kill, words give life; they're either poison or fruit—you choose.

Proverbs 18:21 MSG

EXAMINE

Create a list of five affirmations that can help point you back to God's truth.

....

....

....

....

....

OFFER

God, help me change my language. I pray that my heart, my mind, and my lips would be in one accord and that I would believe the words that flow from my mouth. I believe that goodness and mercy will follow me all the days of my life. In Jesus' name, amen.

26

BUILD YOUR CONFIDENCE

If you're anything like me, Pinterest is your go-to search engine. Whether it's for cute outfit ideas, DIY birthday party decor, or even business advice, there's something refreshing about being able to curate a visual board with all your future goals. Years ago, when I was just starting out in business, I found myself using the platform to find Christian motivational content. God had already impressed on my heart to share encouraging content for Christian business owners, but I wasn't confident that my words would be enough. So for weeks I reshared quotes from others and saved the words that God had given to me *directly* for the caption.

One day that all changed. God gently spoke to me and

said, *If you're busy sharing the messages that I've given everyone else, you're not sharing the message that I've given you.* That really struck something in me. I was unintentionally hiding the words that God had called me to share, all because of my lack of confidence. From that day forward it no longer mattered how uncomfortable or unqualified I felt; I was going to show up and say exactly what God put on my heart—without hiding it. Looking back, and having since reached hundreds of thousands of women who often tell me how much my work impacts them, I now see that God was right all along.

I was unintentionally **hiding the words** that God had called me to share, all because of my **lack of confidence**.

Do you ever find yourself stalling on the thing that God is calling you to do? Whether it's pursuing a new idea, stepping up to serve in ministry, or even sharing your story, you find yourself holding back from making a move because you're not confident that it can be done. Same. And it's not that we're not confident in God; it's that we lack confidence in *ourselves*. We sometimes can't grasp the fact that God would call us to pursue something so far outside our comfort zone.

Here's what I've learned: God often calls us to do things

that require us to step out in faith and partner with Him to make them happen. That means He's going to push you outside the areas where you're comfortable. And as God does this, it's not uncommon for the Enemy to plant seeds of doubt in your mind at the same time.

I don't know how I'm going to pull this off.

Maybe God meant to choose someone else for this.

I should probably stick to what I know.

Here's what I'll tell you: If you truly want to be confident in doing the thing that God is calling you to do, you're going to have to actually step out and do it. Scared or not.

If it's a book He's called you to write, write it.

If it's a business He's called you to launch, launch it.

If it's a new ministry He's called you to create, start it.

If it's a mission trip He wants you to take, go.

When God calls you to step out into new territory, it's for a reason—and that reason is not to set you up for failure, because He has created you with everything you need to succeed in that area. There are people He has assigned to you who are waiting for you to show up.

When God calls you to **step out** into a **new territory**, it's for a reason.

The people you're called to serve aren't expecting you to be perfect—they just need you to show up. And the more you show up, the more confident you'll become. It's simple math.

Like learning to ride a bike, it might be a little rocky in the beginning, and you might have moments when it seems impossible, but if you stick with it, you'll find your confidence and learn to balance and move forward without even having to think about it.

I realize that the thing God is calling you to do may not be as simple as learning to ride a bike, but confidence is a by-product of consistently taking leaps of faith.

Confidence is a by-product of consistently taking **leaps of faith**.

Even if that first step is one where your legs are trembling, one step forward is better than no step at all. And once you've taken enough leaps, you'll notice a huge shift. The abilities that you were once doubtful about you'll now be confident in. In the areas where you were once unsure, you'll now have clarity. And it will no longer matter what challenges come your way because you'll be confident in your calling and ready to handle anything.

CONSIDER

So do not throw away your confidence; it will be richly rewarded.

Hebrews 10:35 NIV

EXAMINE

Do you feel confident in the thing that God has called you to pursue? If not, what are some ways this lack of confidence has impacted your efforts?

....

....

....

....

OFFER

God, I pray that You increase my confidence in the areas where You are calling me to use my gifts. Sometimes the urge to quit is stronger than my urge to keep going, but I ask that You give me the courage to face any obstacles that come my way. I know that You are calling me to step out of my comfort zone, and I am open and ready to follow Your lead. In Jesus' name, amen.

27

TRANSFORM PAIN INTO POWER

My husband and I are both considered tall. He's six foot three and I'm five foot seven, so naturally we expected to have tall children. I remember going to all the annual doctor's appointments for our daughter and seeing how she was always at the top percentile for her height.

As she grew, people would often mistake her for being much older than she actually was. (In fact, they still do.) They'd make comments like, "Wow! She's so tall for her age."

It wasn't until she was about three years old that we experienced a different side of her growing so fast. One night she was in tears, complaining about pain in her legs. We tried every home remedy we could find online, but nothing seemed to work. A few days later, we took her to her pediatrician, and discovered it was growing pains. She grew so much in that year that she was literally feeling the pain of her bones growing in real time. The doctor advised us that the pain would eventually subside, but there was nothing we could do except grow through it.

There are going to be **certain situations** you experience in life that will seem painful in the moment but are **necessary for your growth**.

We typically associate pain with something being wrong, but that's not always the case. There are going to be certain situations you experience in life that will seem painful in the moment but are necessary for your growth.

Sometimes those painful moments can do you just as much good as the pleasurable moments. Experiencing pain is one of the many ways we can build our resilience, because it's in these moments that we learn not only how to manage the pain, but also how to recover, how to push through dark seasons, how to adapt to change, and how to make it to the other side.

And if we can be honest, sometimes it's not even that the experiences are *painful*; they're just uncomfortable. It's a new experience, it's outside our comfort zone, it's stretching us beyond our normal capacity—and those are the times when most people throw in the towel.

But can I tell you something? You're probably a lot closer to the other side than you think. So what if instead of running from the pain, you used it to fuel your fire to keep going?

> Even the **roots of a tree** go through the dirt before the branches ever **make it to sunlight**.

There's a popular meme online of a man digging for diamonds. You can clearly tell that he's been digging for a while based on how lengthy the tunnel is, but within a few feet of hitting the diamonds, he turns around. Arms tired, sweat dripping, and more than likely frustrated, he taps out. He had no idea how close he was to his breakthrough.

You must honor the work you've already done by continuing to move forward. If you quit every time you get uncomfortable, or every time God calls you to the next level, you will surely miss out on what's waiting up ahead.

Even the roots of a tree go through the dirt before the branches ever make it to sunlight. Through the dark moments, through the changing of the seasons, through changes in the environment, the trees continue to grow—and you can too.

CONSIDER

Hard work always pays off; mere talk puts no bread on the table.

Proverbs 14:23 MSG

EXAMINE

What has been your most challenging thing to grow through? How do you cope with change?

....

....

....

....

....

OFFER

God, thank You for all the experiences that help move me forward to the place that You're calling me to. I know it may not always feel good, but it's for my good. I pray that You continue to stretch me so that I can evolve into the woman You're calling me to be. In Jesus' name, amen.

28

TAKE THE RISK AND EMBRACE FAILURE

During my first year of college and for the first time ever, I lived away from home and had to learn to (semi) navigate life on my own. My parents were only a quick phone call away, but there were still some things I experienced daily that I had to learn how to do myself and in real time, like learning to take the campus bus. Before you judge me too hard, I'm not a city girl. Outside of a regular school bus, I had never taken any other form of public transportation.

One day it was pouring rain, and I realized that getting to the other side of campus dry would be nearly impossible. So I decided that day would the day: I was taking the bus, scared and all. I don't know why, but I assumed that the driver would automatically stop at each stop to let people off. I quickly realized that wasn't the case. Too shy to speak up for myself, we passed several stops, and finally I saw another student use the pull cord hanging from the ceiling to signal that they needed to get off. I had completely missed my stop (and several more past it) and ended up right back where I started! It was a risk, albeit small, to take the bus given that I didn't know how to use it, but even through the setbacks, it taught me that things are rarely as bad as we anticipate them to be. A little delayed, but I still made it to my destination.

Things are **rarely as bad** as we **anticipate** them to be.

This often happens to us in life when God gives us a new assignment. There's something He is calling us to do, but day after day, week after week, year after year, we put it on hold. We focus more on the potential outcome than we do on just being obedient and taking the leap. We completely box ourselves in and don't explore all that our gifts and ideas have to offer us.

And if you're like me, you sometimes don't take the leap until it's no longer a gentle nudge but a firm demand. But why? Is it because we're stubborn? Is it because we would rather let life's circumstances guide our steps than follow God's voice? Or is it because we can't get past our own inner thoughts of what might await us on the other side?

Taking risks is a part of the **journey**.

Either way, taking risks is a part of the journey. There's no way around it. But here's the thing: You have to mentally prepare yourself that even if something doesn't work out exactly the way you expect or hope, God can still take it and use it for your good. This isn't to say that you should be naive or reckless in pursuing something without bringing it to God first, nor should you stop pursuing things altogether. Dropping the fear of failure is menat to release you from the fear of taking action.

Whether you're a person who struggles with change or one who has experienced failure after failure after failure, and you're afraid to try again, this is a call for you to shift your perspective. *What's the worst thing that could happen?* I often ask myself this question when being tasked with a new assignment. Ask yourself this enough times, and you'll get down to the *real* reason you're afraid to take the risk.

If your answer is anything along the lines of . . .

I might fail.

I might look crazy.

I might waste my time.

. . . then the worst that can happen isn't really all that bad. On the flip side, I think it's also helpful to ask, *What's the best thing that could happen?* I can guarantee you that *this* list will outweigh everything you mentioned in your worst-case scenario list. And best-case outcomes is the mindset you need to operate from. That's where you find the courage to take the risk.

What's the **best thing** that could happen?

If you ever find yourself struggling to take the leap on something you feel God is calling you to do, I want you to ask yourself these three questions:

Does it glorify God?

Is it a gift that I'm using to serve others or just for my own personal gain?

Do I truly feel a tug from God to pursue it?

If you can confidently answer yes to these questions, you're in a good spot.

In addition, pray for wisdom: *God, help me to make the*

right decisions, but if I ever miss what You've said or if I get it wrong, please guide me back to the place where I'm supposed to be.

I always say it's easier for God to guide your steps when you're *willing* to move your feet. Things may not always turn out the way that you anticipated, but again, God can take whatever you get wrong and make it right. As long as you have a genuine relationship with Him, an ear to hear His voice, and enough faith to keep showing up, all is well. God has the power to reshape every experience, every lesson, every failure, and every setback and make it work for your good.

God has the power to **reshape** every experience and **make it work** for your **good**.

CONSIDER

Let us not grow weary of doing good, for in due season we will reap, if we do not give up.

Galatians 6:9 ESV

EXAMINE

What experiences from your past have felt like rejection but ended up leading you to something better? When was the last time you took a huge leap of faith?

OFFER

God, I thank You for giving me the freedom to explore new ideas and the wisdom to consult with You first. Give me a sensitive ear to hear when You speak and to know when it's time to pivot into what's next. I thank You for protection from the things that I don't know about and for guiding me to what's best. In Jesus' name, amen.

29

SURRENDER TO SUCCEED

I'd like to think I'm pretty consistent when it comes to using my gifts these days, but that wasn't always the case. At one point in time, my lack of understanding about my gifts and true purpose weighed me down like a ton of bricks. I couldn't sleep, I couldn't function at my day job, and I couldn't stop worrying about my future. It all just felt so heavy. Some might even call what I was experiencing depression. Whatever it was, I knew I had to face it and work my way through it.

My daily prayer at that time was, *God, if You could just remove this weight and tell me what it is I'm supposed to be doing, I'll gladly do it every day*. But He didn't answer that prayer right away, nor did He give me the complete answer all at once. In fact, He's still revealing what's next for me. Looking back I truly believe that the wait was directly tied to the posture of my heart. I was so focused on what I was supposed to be doing that I neglected the most important thing: building a relationship with God, no strings attached.

We get so caught up in the **day-to-day** that we miss out on what this **entire journey** is about.

Oftentimes we find ourselves in the cycle of trying to prove we have purpose, whether it's to ourselves, our peers, or even strangers. We get so caught up in the day-to-day that we miss out on what this entire journey is about.

Yes, we should be pursuing the things that God calls us to do, but not at the expense of our relationship with Him. God does not give us gifts, talents, and ideas to pull us further away from Him but rather to draw us closer. If we are constantly on this hamster wheel, rushing our way through life, it's possible that we may be creating our own roadblocks.

We will forever feel disconnected from our purpose if we are pursuing the gift but neglecting the One who gave it to us. And here's what we can know with certainty: When we focus on building our relationship with God first, everything else will fall into place.

The gifts start making room (Proverbs 18:16).

The ideas start flowing (Proverbs 2:6)

And before we know it, God is answering prayer requests that never even left our lips because He knows our *heart*. He can see that we're in a good place, that we're going to be wise stewards of whatever He gives us access to, and that we are prioritizing Him over everything else.

Your **relationship** with God is the **glue** that holds everything together.

Listen, if you've ever felt like you've been doing the thing that God called you to do but you're not seeing the progress that you thought you would, you're not alone. I want to challenge you to slow down and get back to the basics.

Slowing down doesn't necessarily mean you have to quit altogether. Instead, reprogram your mind with the truth that your relationship with God is most important. The success will come and so will the answered prayers.

For what it's worth, you don't have to prove that you have a purpose. God has already confirmed that from the

Stay connected to Him.

very beginning. No matter where you are in your journey, just know that your relationship with God is the glue that holds everything together and the key that unlocks every door with your name on it. Stay connected to Him.

CONSIDER

"You shall love the Lord your God with all your heart and with all your soul and with all your mind. This is the great and first commandment."

Matthew 22:37–38 ESV

EXAMINE

Do you focus on your relationship with God just as much as you focus on pursuing your dreams? If not, what are some ways you can change that?

....

....

....

....

....

OFFER

God, please remove anything from my heart that is not like You. Give me the desire to prioritize my relationship with You before anything else. I know that when I am in alignment with You, everything else will fall into place. In Jesus' name, amen.

30

PRIORITIZE GOD OVER EXPECTATIONS

My youngest daughter, Sydney, is the ultimate risk taker. It's rare to see her back down from a challenge.

We recently discovered a new park in our neighborhood, and the moment she spotted the dome-shaped structure with ropes that are intertwined like a spiderweb, her eyes lit up.

I've been known to take a risk or two in my lifetime, but something about watching *my kids* take risks causes me to panic. Who would've thought?

So little Miss Sydney decided she wanted to try out the

spider climber. Not wanting to discourage her, I told her to try it, but I offered her instructions to stay at the bottom where it was safe. She hopped on and almost immediately headed straight for the top. At that point, I was up and walking toward her, encouraging (more like scolding) her to come back down.

She ignored me and kept climbing, and before I knew it, I was shouting, "You're going to fall! Be careful! Don't swing like that! Watch your step!" Eventually I stopped, realizing she really *did* have the hang of this. It was a good thing she didn't let me push my fears onto her.

How many times have we been in situations where we **shared our dreams and goals** with people only to have them put doubts and fears in our mind?

How many times have we been in situations where we shared our dreams and goals with people only to have them put doubts and fears in our mind that weren't originally there?

"That's already been done before."

"Aren't you afraid of failing?"

"What if you waste your time and money?"

Before we know it, confidence is replaced with discouragement, and we allow it to negatively impact how we show up.

Fear is contagious, but so is confidence. And this is why

it's important to surround yourself with other dreamers—other people who know that without risk, there is no reward. People who know that the vision you're pursuing is bigger than you. Because even in your moments of unbelief, there's nothing like having somebody on your team rooting for you to finish the race.

> In times of struggle **you need people in your corner** who will encourage you to keep going.

This reminds me of the story in Exodus 17:8–13 when Moses went to the mountaintop with Aaron and Hur. There was a battle happening, and every time Moses raised his hands, the Israelites started winning, but when he lowered them, the Amalekites started winning. Seeing how tired he was, Aaron and Hur gave him a stone to sit on and held up his arms for him, one on each side.

It wasn't even necessarily their assignment, but Aaron and Hur were still willing to support Moses so he could complete what *he* was called to do.

In times of struggle you need people in your corner who, at the very least, will encourage you to keep going. It does you no good to listen to the doubts and fears of others or to engage in conversations that work against your calling.

I realize that not everyone has an Aaron or a Hur in their

corner, but even if you don't have a person to turn to right now, remember that you can *always* turn to God.

You can tell Him when you're tired.

You can tell Him when you're afraid.

You can tell Him when you just need an extra moment to breathe.

You can tell Him that you desire to have godly connections with like-minded people.

Just as Jesus provided support for Moses, He can do it for you too.

CONSIDER

Whoever walks with the wise becomes wise, but the companion of fools will suffer harm.

Proverbs 13:20 ESV

EXAMINE

Have you ever allowed anyone to talk you out of something you know God called you to do? How careful are you when sharing your God-given dreams with others?

....

....

....

....

OFFER

God, surround me with the right people who will have a positive impact on my life. Increase my discernment so I can identify anyone sent to instill fear or doubt. I pray that You block anything that attempts to interfere with my purpose from You. In Jesus' name, amen.

31

BE AUTHENTIC

When I first joined the online space, I had zero clue about which direction to take. All I knew was that I wanted to use my voice. I didn't know what that looked like, so I started doing market research and finding people who were having success in the areas I wanted to explore. And that was the introduction to me second-guessing myself and my ideas.

One minute I was focused on pursuing the vision God had given me, and the next I was scrapping the whole thing and doing what seemed popular. Even though the popular thing didn't really interest me, I wanted the success I saw others experiencing, so I went with it anyway.

Speaking from experience here, the quickest way to burn yourself out is to go against who you truly feel called to be. I know we don't pick up these habits with the intention of being inauthentic or copying our peers, but when we see what's working for everyone else, it's easy to think it'll also work for us. But that isn't always the case.

This isn't to say that God can't call us to do multiple things or that we shouldn't be inspired by our peers who are also walking in their calling, but we should never allow inspiration to become a distraction. More often than not the thing that God calls us to do isn't going to be what's popular. In fact, it might be the complete opposite. And as hard as that may be to understand, it's even harder to build something that isn't in alignment with who we are at our core.

We should never allow **inspiration** to become a **distraction**.

Do you know how hard it is to force yourself into the places where you don't fit? Extremely. Thankfully, God has already created a place where you can thrive. A place where you won't have to "fake it to make it."

Your calling is not a stage play. It's not something that you have to put on display and *perform*. Your calling is a true reflection of who God already created you to be. And the more you run from your true calling, the more unnecessary pressure you put on yourself. You end up changing the way you speak, the way you look, the way you write, the opportunities you pursue, and so on. And then you wonder why you have deep feelings of dissatisfaction. It's simply because you are holding yourself to a standard that's not even meant for you.

> Sometimes God will call you to go **left** when everyone else is going **right**.

Here's what I want you to consider: There is a specific message and gift that God has entrusted you with and there are specific people who have been assigned to you. Your uniqueness is what will draw them in, but if you are spending your time trying to camouflage yourself among everyone else, you may never stand out in the way you're supposed to.

Sometimes God will call you to go left when everyone else is going right, and your desire to fit in should not be greater than your desire for obedience.

Remember, God knows you at your core, and He has given you gifts and ideas to complement who you are. Don't make it harder on yourself than it needs to be.

Be authentic and stick to what He has called *you* to pursue. The people assigned to you are waiting.

CONSIDER

For we are God's handiwork, created in Christ Jesus to do good works, which God prepared in advance for us to do.

Ephesians 2:10 NIV

EXAMINE

Do you struggle with following the instructions that God has given you when they're different from what everyone else is doing? What steps can you take to eliminate distractions?

....

....

....

....

OFFER

God, please do not allow me to be easily distracted by what I see others doing. I know that You created me with my own set of gifts and talents, and I trust that they will make room for me wherever I go. Help me to show up authentically as the woman You have created me to be. In Jesus' name, amen.

32

EMBRACE DIVINE ORDER

Back in 2020 my husband and I decided it was time to purchase a new home. With a growing family, we knew we needed more space. So right in the thick of the pandemic, we put our house on the market and started searching for the perfect home.

After touring several neighborhoods, we decided that a new build was our best option. The day they finally cleared the land was the first moment we could truly say, "Wow, this is really happening!" The first thing they did after clearing the land was lay the basement foundation. Next, they did the framing, and then they built the main level. The outside framing of the house went up fast, but when it came time for the smaller details, things slowed down a bit.

One thing I noticed during that process was that nothing arrived onsite before it was needed. From having only a machine to clear the land, to a concrete pourer, to lumber, to drywall, to doors and windows, to hardware, to siding and brick, everything arrived and left exactly when it was supposed to and not a minute sooner.

> Even though **we are believers**, and we're instructed to operate in **faith**, sometimes it's hard for us to **see** what we can't actually *see.*

We experience this same phenomenon in our lives. When we're building something new but we're struggling to see how things will turn out in the end, we start wondering when we're going to get more—whether that's time, resources, connections, or whatever else.

We start wondering if what we have is enough, as if God doesn't know what we need.

We start picking things apart and building a false narrative. Go figure.

Even though we are believers and we're instructed to operate in faith, sometimes it's hard for us to see what we can't actually *see*. We are often looking at our spiritual assignment through our natural lenses.

Our natural *mind* tells us we need more resources.

Our natural *eyes* tell us things aren't adding up.

Our natural *feelings* make us question if things are going to work.

This is exactly why the Bible tells us to lean not on our own understanding (Proverbs 3:5–6). Whenever we pursue gifts and ideas from God, it will always be in our best interest to shift our mindset and to view things from a spiritual perspective.

The good news is that God knows exactly what we need to fulfill the vision that He has placed on our heart. Not only that, He also knows how to line up the pieces so that everything will arrive exactly when it's supposed to. We need to trust that whatever we need is already in motion.

Had the builders working on our home scheduled the supplies to be delivered all at once, they would've had more than they could handle in that moment, limiting their space and ability to move freely on the property. That would've been more of a hindrance than a help. To avoid this problem, they put in purchase orders for various supplies for specific arrival dates. And even though they couldn't see it, they knew the materials that they needed were on the way.

My challenge to you today is to focus on what's already been delivered. Focus on what God has given you in *this* moment. Because the more time you spend scrutinizing your current situation, the more likely you are to miss what's already in your possession.

Don't quit during the **building** phase.

Chances are there's a purchase order out there that already has your name on it, along with a delivery date you know nothing about. Don't quit during the building phase. *More* is on the way.

CONSIDER

"When the right time comes, I the LORD will quickly do this!"

Isaiah 60:22 NET

EXAMINE

What is one promise you have been waiting on the Lord to fulfill? Has this had any impact on your confidence in God's timing?

OFFER

God, I know Your timing is perfect. Help me to see the good in every season, even the seasons of waiting. I trust that the things You have promised me have my name on them and will arrive exactly when they're supposed to. In Jesus' name, amen.

33

SURRENDER CONTROL

After spending a week at Disney World, my family and I were finally headed back home. The trip had been amazing. We'd walked, eaten, laughed, swum, explored, and walked some more. It was a much-needed getaway! You'll probably agree when I say this, but it's always bittersweet for me when vacations end. It's back to the real world when you get home, but you're also ready to get back on schedule.

As we boarded the plane for home, the sun was shining without a cloud in sight. It wasn't until we were halfway through our flight that the pilot announced over the loudspeaker that turbulence that was ahead. I've been on plenty of flights, so I wasn't too fazed by this announcement, but that first jolt of turbulence that night made me feel differently. I was no longer calm, cool, and collected. I was anxiously staring at my husband and holding on to our daughter as tightly as I could.

What may seem like the **end of the world** to us is only a **small thing** to God.

With my heart nearly beating out of my chest, I realized that prayer and surrender were the only (and best) things I could do. *God is in control.* That's what I kept telling myself until we had passed through the storm.

Sometimes in life we experience stressful situations that are beyond our control and we forget that we can surrender our worries to God. What may seem like the end of the world to us is only a small thing to God.

The stressful job.

The unsuccessful business launch.

The stifled ministry growth.

The failed idea.

The broken relationship.

We become frustrated, worried, and overwhelmed.

But what do you think would happen if you were to release some of those things that are causing you stress, anxiety, and worry and just surrender them to God?

What do you think would happen if you stopped expecting things to be perfect and trusted God with the outcome?

The truth is, there will always be things that are out of your control—always. The only thing you have any control over is your willingness to keep showing up. You have to make the decision to surrender everything beyond that to God. The outcome of the business? It's up to God. The opportunities that come your way? Up to God. The amount of time that it takes for everything to come to fruition? All up to God.

Knowing that **God is working** just as hard on your behalf as you are **does something for the soul**.

You see, even though God gives us the assignment, He's not tasking us with managing the results. Our obedience is enough.

And no, this doesn't mean to reduce your efforts; it simply means you surrender everything outside your control to God, allowing Him to add His *super* to your *natural*.

Once you do that, here's what you'll start to notice: The burden that you've placed on yourself will become lighter. That doesn't necessarily mean that the journey will be easy, but knowing that God is working just as hard on your behalf as you are does something for the soul.

When you give God your worries, *really* give them to Him.

When you release control, you give yourself the opportunity to see God's hand at work in your life.

He can take every mistake and make it right.

He can take every loss and make it a win.

He can take every struggle and make it a victory.

He is able to do exceedingly, abundantly above all that we think or ask (Ephesians 3:20). So even when you experience unexpected situations, surrender the outcome to God, trying your best not to micromanage, and trust that everything will work out for your good—because it will.

Trust that **everything will work** out for your good—because it will.

CONSIDER

Now to him who is able to do far more abundantly than all that we ask or think, according to the power at work within us.

Ephesians 3:20 ESV

EXAMINE

How has holding yourself responsible for the outcome affected the way you show up? What can you surrender to God in this season?

....

....

....

....

....

OFFER

God, I surrender to You everything that's outside of my control. I believe that You see the effort I am putting in, and I trust that everything will work out exactly how it's supposed to. I trust that even in the areas where I fall short, You will come in and make them whole. In Jesus' name, amen.

PART 4 WRAP-UP

ACTION PLAN TO FIND THE COURAGE TO MOVE FORWARD

You made it to the end! But before we celebrate, let's do one final wrap-up. By now you've learned that courage isn't always something we build overnight. It's something we must actively pursue.

Whether we do that by taking risks, embracing failures, or even surrounding ourselves with the right people, the more we push ourselves beyond our comfort zone, the quicker we can build our courage.

When you really stop and think about it, courage and faith go hand in hand. You may not always see the full picture, but when you have faith in God and know what *He* can do, you'll have the courage you need to move forward.

Your journey may not be perfect, but that's okay. You've got to be willing to give yourself the opportunity to explore what God has placed in your heart. The less you focus on fear, or potentially making a wrong move, or things that are beyond your control, the more time you'll have to focus on the task at hand.

As I've said before, God is not looking for perfection; He's looking for obedience.

There are three phases to moving forward in courage:

Phase 1: You psych yourself up to take the leap. You still feel the fear, but you mentally prepare yourself to take action.

Phase 2: You're approaching the point of taking action, and you are putting your practice into motion. You're doing all the things to build your confidence, but you might still be experiencing a little bit of hesitation, and you're comforted by the fact that there's still time to turn back. (Honestly, this is where most people jump ship.)

Phase 3: This is when you finally put the pedal to the metal. In this phase, it's go time. Scared or not, there's no holding back. And this is the scariest phase of them all, but it's also the most *necessary*.

What phase do you think best describes your current season?

Are you gearing yourself up to take the leap?

Are you putting your practice into motion?

Or are you at the point of taking action?

No matter what season you're in, just know that if God called you to do it, the ball is in your court to muster up the courage and get it done.

Take some time to work through the following action steps.

STEP #1: WHAT RISK HAVE YOU BEEN AFRAID TO TAKE?

There's always one thing that we know we should've done a long time ago, but we sit on it out of fear or the naive belief that we have more time. But that risk you're afraid to take could be the very thing that'll open you up to new levels beyond what you can dream of. And no, it doesn't always have to be something drastic. Sometimes that first step is just enough to get you to leave your comfort zone and get the momentum going.

STEP #2: HOW CAN YOU SHIFT YOUR PERSPECTIVE WHEN IT COMES TO FAILURE?

I don't know what it is about failure, but most people you talk to would skip it if they had the option. But I want to challenge you to shift your perspective when it comes to how you respond to failure.

Some of us assume that because we are pursuing God-given gifts and ideas, we are exempt from failure, but this couldn't be further from the truth. Sometimes failure is the very thing that God will use to build our character, increase our faith, sharpen our skills, or even to strengthen our prayer life.

In every failure there's a lesson—even if it's just knowing what *not* to do moving forward. Because I promise you, if you fail enough times and apply that information to each new adventure, it's only a matter of time before you hit it out of the park.

STEP #3: HOW FREQUENTLY ARE YOU SPEAKING POSITIVELY TO YOURSELF?

Sometimes we can be our own worst critic. We speak to ourselves in ways we'd never talk to others. That alone becomes a huge issue when it comes to acting on those things that God has assigned you. If you're constantly telling yourself that you're unqualified or not good enough, it's going to be that much tougher to show up. Change your words, and you can literally change your life.

CONCLUSION

It's time to celebrate! You made it through an entire book designed to help you pursue all that God has put in your heart. But the journey doesn't stop here. In fact, it's just getting started.

Now that you have a new outlook on how to show up for the things you feel called to do, I pray that your steps stay aligned with God's in this next chapter of your life. Don't rush ahead of Him, but also don't procrastinate or move too slowly. Find your rhythm. I pray that you give yourself grace when you make mistakes and that you put forth your best effort in everything you do. I pray that you

Life is not **linear**.

allow yourself to experience human emotions and also know when to fight negativity with God's Word.

And more than anything, I want you to remember that God has a purpose for your life. In some seasons, that purpose will be clear, and other seasons may come with a little more rain than sunshine; but in all seasons, God is good, and He has a plan.

Life is not linear. It's ever evolving, full of ebbs and flows. If you keep going, you'll keep your momentum, and you'll know how to keep going in the hard seasons instead of allowing them to consume you.

> I pray that you walk away from this book feeling **hopeful**, **confident**, and **ready** to tackle the task God has assigned to you.

Remember, God didn't say we won't face mountains in our lives; He told us that if we have faith, we can speak to the mountain and tell it to move (Mark 11:23). And *that* is what I want you to hold on to. You'll never encounter an obstacle that you can't command to move in Jesus' name.

God has good things in store not only for you but also for the people who will be impacted by your obedience. All it takes is one idea, one ministry, one book, one business, one move to change everything. So whatever it is that God has placed in your heart, pursue it.

Without seeking external validation.

Without continuously asking God for more signs when He's already given you the green light.

Without allowing fear to consume your thoughts.

Will it be an adjustment in the beginning? Absolutely. But I promise that if you keep going, you'll make it to the other side. And I don't mean "keep going" in a toxic way where you're not allowed to rest; I'm talking about simply sticking with God through it all. Whether that's stepping outside of your comfort zone, pivoting when necessary, or even going back to the drawing board when you've gotten too far off track, don't lose your fight.

And don't be surprised if there are seasons when God is calling you to rest. For some of us, we confuse rest with quitting, but that couldn't be further from the truth. Psalm 127:2 (THE VOICE) says, "*God provides for His own.* It is pointless to get up early, *work hard,* and go to bed late anxiously laboring for food to eat; for God provides for those He loves, even while they are sleeping." In other words, you don't have to burn yourself out trying to prove your obedience to God. He sees it. And even when you're not working, *He still is.*

No matter what season you're in, I pray that you know that the unique gifts and ideas you bring to this world are needed. And I pray that these personal stories have given you insight on how to move forward with all God is calling you to do. I pray that you walk away feeling hopeful, confident, and ready to tackle the task God has assigned to you.

Now, you know I can't let you go without closing this out in prayer, right?

God, I thank You for every reader who has picked up this book. I pray that the words on these pages have not only encouraged her but that they will continue to touch her heart. I pray that her confidence is strengthened, her faith is increased, and more importantly, her walk with You becomes closer than ever. I pray that You continue to guide her steps as she goes out and pursues the dreams and ideas that You have placed in her heart. Remind her that she is called and equipped for greatness. In Jesus' name, amen.

With love,

TANESHIA

ACKNOWLEDGMENTS

To my editors, Jessica Lamb, Stephanie Newton, and Bonnie Honeycutt, thank you for your unwavering dedication, keen eyes, and thoughtful guidance. Your expertise helped me write this devotional with clarity and heart.

To my agent, Stephanie Tresner, thank you for believing in me and in this project from the very beginning. Not only did you help me navigate the journey of publishing, but you also reminded me to trust the process and my own voice along the way.

TANESHIA YERBY is a wife, a mother, a writer, and the founder of Christian Entrepreneur Organization, an online community that gives women of faith practical guidance on how to pursue their God-given purpose. She has a degree in communications from Norfolk State University in Norfolk, Virginia.